YOUR
SONGS OF
PRAISE

With notes by

F. COLQUHOUN
Author of 'A Hymn Companion'
Hodder & Stoughton

and a foreword by

R. ROYLE

Illustrations by

R. HUBBARD

OXFORD UNIVERSITY PRESS
BBC BOOKS · 1987

Published by
Oxford University Press, Walton Street, Oxford OX2 6DP

Oxford New York Toronto
Delhi Bombay Calcutta Madras Karachi
Petaling Jaya Singapore Hong Kong Tokyo
Nairobi Dar es Salaam Cape Town
Melbourne Auckland

and associated companies in
Berlin Ibadan

Oxford is a trade mark of Oxford University Press

BBC Books
A division of BBC Enterprises Ltd
Woodlands
80 Wood Lane
London W12 0TT

First printed in 1987
Reprinted 1992

ISBN 0 19 143321 7 (OUP)
ISBN 0 563 20571 7 (BBC)

Printed in Great Britain by
J. W. Arrowsmith Ltd,
Bristol

Foreword

The hymn 'Abide with me' is the only link I know between a peaceful evening service and a rowdy, excitable Cup Final crowd. But do you know which hymn binds the Women's Institute with Eton College? It is 'Jerusalem'. This vision of Blake's, set to music by Parry, is sung by both organizations on important occasions in their calendars.

Hymns have this wonderful power of bringing people together. Christians, divided by doctrine and organization, will come together for hymns. That 'all-purpose' hymn 'The Lord's my Shepherd', which joins Christians with Jews, can unite people in the happiness of marriage and comfort them in the sorrow of a funeral.

The very best hymns lift us out of ourselves, so that as we sing 'Holy, Holy, Holy' we are joined with the heavenly choir who, day and night, sing praises to God. It is only when hymns are sung to a different tune from the one that we know and love, the 'proper' tune, as we like to call it, that they become divisive.

For over twenty-five years *Songs of Praise* has been a programme that has brought people together. From the letters I receive and the comments I hear, many people, including the elderly and house-bound, look forward to the programme. It links them with their friends who they know will also be watching. It also links the housebound with their Churches and Chapels which, through disability, they are often no longer able to attend.

Although many of us are creatures of habit and like the familiar, for me one of the excitements of *Songs of Praise* is that it joins us with the new, the unfamiliar. New choruses, Black Gospel music, the music of the Synagogue, have all been ear-openers to me, and I know that many of you have enjoyed the experience of looking outside your own familiar world.

By travelling the length and breadth of the British Isles, *Songs of Praise* brings back memories of favourite seaside resorts, marvellous holidays, particular friendships, and manages to unite us as a nation—with the occasional reminder that we are part of a world community as well.

Those of you who have attended a recording of the hymns for *Songs of Praise* will know what hard work it is, but from now on you have no excuse not to join in. The one hundred hymns in this book are those most regularly requested and sung on the programme. With this book in front of you, you will also be able to offer to God your Songs of Praise.

August 1986   ROGER ROYLE

Acknowledgements

Oxford University Press wishes to thank the following who have given permission for copyright material to be included:

Author	Permission granted by	Hymn No.
Appleford, P.	Josef Weinberger Ltd.	52
Bell, G. K. A.	Oxford University Press	16
Bennard, G.	Word (UK) Ltd.	89
Brooks, R. T.	Oxford University Press	81
Burns, E. J.	Author	96
Carter, S.	Stainer & Bell Ltd.	54
Chisholm, T. O.	Hope Publishing Company	29
Dudley-Smith, T.	Author	83
Farjeon, E.	David Higham Associates	58
Hine, S.	Thankyou Music Ltd.	67
Hoyle, R. B. (*tr.*)	World Student Christian Federation	91
Lafferty, K.	Word (UK) Ltd.	80
Newbolt, M. R. (*tr.*)	Hymns Ancient & Modern Ltd.	48
Petti, A. G. (*adpt.*)	Faber Music Ltd.	34
Smith, L. E.	Thankyou Music Ltd.	75
Struther, J.	Oxford University Press	53
Temple, S.	Franciscan Communications Centre, USA	56

Your Favourite Songs of Praise

1 *Abide with me*

Abide with me; fast falls the eventide:
The darkness deepens; Lord, with me abide;
When other helpers fail, and comforts flee,
Help of the helpless, O abide with me.

2

Swift to its close ebbs out life's little day;
Earth's joys grow dim, its glories pass away;
Change and decay in all around I see;
O thou who changest not, abide with me.

3

I need thy presence every passing hour;
What but thy grace can foil the tempter's power?
Who like thyself my guide and stay can be?
Through cloud and sunshine, O abide with me.

4

I fear no foe, with thee at hand to bless;
Ills have no weight, and tears no bitterness;
Where is death's sting? Where, grave, thy victory?
I triumph still, if thou abide with me.

5

Hold thou thy Cross before my closing eyes;
Shine through the gloom, and point me to the skies:
Heaven's morning breaks, and earth's vain shadows
    flee;
In life, in death, O Lord, abide with me.

Henry Francis Lyte (1793–1847)

Henry Francis Lyte was a dying man when he wrote this hymn, and he knew it. The words 'fast falls the eventide' refer not to the close of day but to the evening of life.

For twenty-five years he had been vicar of the Devonshire fishing village of Brixham. Now, at the age of 54, his health had broken and he was preparing to leave for the south of France.

His immortal hymn was written shortly before his departure from Brixham. He died of consumption at Nice a few weeks later.

Not surprisingly then, this is a hymn about death. But still more it is a hymn about *faith*— the sort of faith that faces death triumphantly and without fear.

2 All hail the power of Jesus' name

All hail the power of Jesus' name,
    Let angels prostrate fall;
Bring forth the royal diadem,
    And crown him Lord of all.

2

Crown him, ye morning stars of light,
    Who fixed this floating ball,
Now hail the strength of Israel's might,
    And crown him Lord of all.

3

Ye seed of Israel's chosen race,
    Ye ransomed of the Fall;
Hail him who saves you by his grace,
    And crown him Lord of all.

4

Hail him, ye heirs of David's line,
    Whom David Lord did call;
The God incarnate, Man divine,
    And crown him Lord of all.

5

Sinners, whose love can ne'er forget
  The wormwood and the gall;
Go spread your trophies at his feet,
  And crown him Lord of all.

6

Let every tribe and every tongue
  Before him prostrate fall;
And shout in universal song
  The crownèd Lord of all.

Edward Perronet (1726–92)

Edward Perronet's father was a parson and an intimate friend of John and Charles Wesley. Thus his son early fell under the spell of the two brothers and shared closely in their evangelical work.

Later, however, disillusioned with the Church of England, he parted from them, turned Dissenter, and became minister of a small chapel in Canterbury.

It was during this time that he wrote his fine 'Coronation Hymn', as it has been called. It has gone through a good many alterations and additions, but the hymn's grand design remains the same: to affirm the kingship of Jesus and call upon the whole of creation to 'crown him Lord of all'.

3 All my hope on God is founded

All my hope on God is founded;
  He doth still my trust renew,
Me through change and chance he guideth,
  Only good and only true.
      God unknown,
      He alone
Calls my heart to be his own.

2

Pride of man and earthly glory,
  Sword and crown betray his trust;
What with care and toil he buildeth,
  Tower and temple, fall to dust.
      But God's power,
      Hour by hour,
Is my temple and my tower.

3

God's great goodness aye endureth,
  Deep his wisdom, passing thought:
Splendour, light, and life attend him,
  Beauty springeth out of naught.
      Evermore
      From his store
New-born worlds rise and adore.

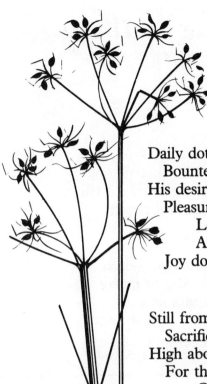

4

Daily doth the^almighty giver
  Bounteous gifts on us bestow;
His desire our soul delighteth,
  Pleasure leads us where we go.
    Love doth stand
    At his hand;
  Joy doth wait on his command.

5

Still from man to God eternal
  Sacrifice of praise be done,
High above all praises praising
  For the gift of Christ his Son.
    Christ doth call
    One and all:
  Ye who follow shall not fall.

Joachim Neander (1650–80)
Par. Robert Bridges (1844–1930)

Dr Robert Bridges, who in middle life abandoned medicine for literature, became Poet Laureate in 1912. He published this hymn a few years earlier.

It is said to be based on the work of the German hymn-writer Joachim Neander (see no. 78). In fact Neander's verses did little more than suggest the theme: faith in *God*, not in 'man and earthly glory'. In one form or another this note runs through the whole hymn.

Its present popularity is largely due to the fine tune *Michael* which Herbert Howells composed for it in 1930. It took him only a few minutes to write, he said. He named it after his son, who died in childhood.

4 *All people that on earth do dwell*

All people that on earth do dwell,
   Sing to the Lord with cheerful voice;
Him serve with mirth, his praise forth tell,
   Come ye before him and rejoice.

2

Know that the Lord is God indeed;
   Without our aid he did us make;
We are his folk, he doth us feed;
   And for his sheep he doth us take.

3

O enter then his gates with praise,
    Approach with joy his courts unto;
Praise, laud, and bless his name always,
    For it is seemly so to do.

4

For why, the Lord our God is good:
    His mercy is for ever sure;
His truth at all times firmly stood,
    And shall from age to age endure.

William Kethe (d. 1594)

This magnificent paraphrase of Psalm 100, first published in Geneva in 1560, is the earliest of the old metrical psalms to find a place in our hymn-books.

Its author William Kethe was an Anglican clergyman who, like many Protestants at the time, took refuge from persecution on the Continent. He spent the last part of his life as rector of the Dorset village of Childe Okeford.

The hymn's famous tune *Old Hundredth* belongs to the same period (1551). Both words and music must have been as familiar to Shakespeare and the great Elizabethans as they are to us.

5 *All things bright and beautiful*

All things bright and beautiful,
  All creatures great and small,
All things wise and wonderful,
  The Lord God made them all.

2

Each little flower that opens,
  Each little bird that sings,
He made their glowing colours,
  He made their tiny wings:

3

The purple-headed mountain,
  The river running by,
The sunset, and the morning
  That brightens up the sky:

4

The cold wind in the winter,
The pleasant summer sun,
The ripe fruits in the garden,
He made them every one:

5

He gave us eyes to see them,
And lips that we might tell
How great is God Almighty
Who has made all things well:

Cecil Frances Alexander (1818–95)

Mrs Cecil Frances Alexander, probably the foremost Irish hymn-writer, published her *Hymns for Little Children* in 1848, a year or two before her marriage to a leading Irish clergyman.

Her design in this book was to make the articles of the Apostles' Creed more intelligible to children by the use of poetry and picture language.

The present hymn illustrates the doctrine of Creation. God is the Maker of all that is good in the world. Flowers and birds, trees and meadows, mountains and rivers—'the Lord God *made* them all.' That verb is the key to the entire hymn.

See also no. 90.

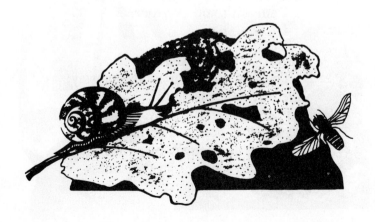

6 *Alleluia! sing to Jesus*

Alleluia! sing to Jesus,
  His the sceptre, his the throne;
Alleluia! his the triumph,
  His the victory alone:
Hark! the songs of peaceful Zion
  Thunder like a mighty flood;
Jesus out of every nation
  Hath redeemed us by his blood.

2

Alleluia! not as orphans
  Are we left in sorrow now;
Alleluia! he is near us,
  Faith believes, nor questions how:
Though the cloud from sight received him
  When the forty days were o'er,
Shall our hearts forget his promise,
  'I am with you evermore'?

3

Alleluia! bread of angels,
  Thou on earth our food, our stay;
Alleluia! here the sinful
  Flee to thee from day to day;
Intercessor, friend of sinners,
  Earth's Redeemer, plead for me,
Where the songs of all the sinless
  Sweep across the crystal sea.

Alleluia! King eternal,
    Thee the Lord of lords we own;
Alleluia! born of Mary,
    Earth thy footstool, heaven thy throne:
Thou within the veil hast entered,
    Robed in flesh, our great High Priest;
Thou on earth both priest and victim
    In the Eucharistic feast.

William Chatterton Dix (1837–98)

Unlike most hymn-writers William Chatterton Dix was a layman. The son of a Bristol surgeon and a devout Anglican, he was for many years manager of a marine insurance company in Glasgow.

He wrote many hymns, including 'As with gladness men of old' for the Epiphany. The present one is a communion hymn which he composed for the festival of the Ascension.

'Alleluia'—the Hebrew word with which each verse begins—is an expression of praise to God. The whole hymn rings with praise and is a celebration of Christ as our Redeemer and King.

7 *Amazing grace*

Amazing grace (how sweet the sound)
   That saved a wretch like me!
I once was lost, but now am found,
   Was blind, but now I see.

2

Through many dangers, toils and snares
   I have already come;
God's grace has brought me safe thus far,
   And he will lead me home.

3

The Lord has promised good to me,
   His word my hope secures;
He will my shield and portion be
   As long as life endures.

4

And, when this heart and flesh shall fail
   And mortal life shall cease,
I shall possess within the veil
   A life of joy and peace.

John Newton (1725–1807)

This hymn is a piece of spiritual autobiography. Its author John Newton, one-time captain of a slave-ship and on his own confession 'an infidel and libertine', had experienced a remarkable conversion.

It so thoroughly changed him that the one-time 'wretch' became a clergyman and served the parish of Olney, Bucks, where he wrote his many hymns.

He tells us how the change happened in this hymn. It was not his own doing. It was all due to God's 'amazing grace': his free, unmerited, unlimited love for sinners like Newton himself. That was why the word 'grace' sounded so sweetly to him, as did also the name of Jesus (see no. 36).

8 *And can it be that I should gain*

And can it be, that I should gain
 An interest in the Saviour's blood?
Died he for me, who caused his pain—
 For me, who him to death pursued?
Amazing love! how can it be
That thou, my God, shouldst die for me?

2

He left his Father's throne above,—
 So free, so infinite his grace—
Emptied himself of all but love,
 And bled for Adam's helpless race:
'Tis mercy all, immense and free;
For, O my God, it found out me!

3

Long my imprisoned spirit lay
 Fast bound in sin and nature's night;
Thine eye diffused a quickening ray—
 I woke, the dungeon flamed with light;
My chains fell off, my heart was free,
I rose, went forth, and followed thee.

No condemnation now I dread;
　　Jesus, and all in him, is mine!
Alive in him, my living Head,
　　And clothed in righteousness divine,
Bold I approach the eternal throne,
And claim the crown, through Christ my own.

Charles Wesley (1707–88)

Many Christians, especially Methodists, would place this among their favourite hymns. Charles Wesley wrote it shortly after his evangelical conversion, which happened on Whit Sunday 1738.

The hymn perfectly expresses his sense of wonder and gratitude at the transformation that then took place in his life when he became a 'born again' Christian.

But note that in writing of this deep spiritual experience Wesley is by no means wrapped up in himself. He is absorbed even more by the 'amazing love' of Christ for him personally and by his discovery of God's 'Free Grace'—the title he gave the hymn when it was published in 1739.

9 And did those feet in ancient time

And did those feet in ancient time
   Walk upon England's mountains green?
And was the holy Lamb of God
   On England's pleasant pastures seen?
And did the countenance divine
   Shine forth upon our clouded hills?
And was Jerusalem builded here
   Among those dark satanic mills?

2

Bring me my bow of burning gold!
   Bring me my arrows of desire!
Bring me my spear! O clouds, unfold!
   Bring me my chariot of fire!
I will not cease from mental fight,
   Nor shall my sword sleep in my hand,
Till we have built Jerusalem
   In England's green and pleasant land.

William Blake (1757–1827)

William Blake's famous lyric comes from the preface to his work *Milton*, published in 1804.

In mystical and highly symbolical language—by no means easy to understand—it is a challenge to the nation to fight against all social evils which repress man's freedom. In fact it is a call to make England a new Jerusalem, a little heaven on earth.

The lines remained virtually unknown for over a century. Then in 1916 Sir Hubert Parry's magnificent tune *Jerusalem* (which he wrote for it to celebrate women's suffrage) set the obscure words alight and created a hymn which has become a second national anthem.

10 *At the name of Jesus*

At the name of Jesus
  Every knee shall bow,
Every tongue confess him
  King of glory now;
'Tis the Father's pleasure
  We should call him Lord,
Who from the beginning
  Was the mighty Word.

2

Humbled for a season,
  To receive a name
From the lips of sinners
  Unto whom he came,
Faithfully he bore it
  Spotless to the last;
Brought it back victorious,
  When from death he passed.

3

In your hearts enthrone him;
   There let him subdue
All that is not holy,
   All that is not true:
Crown him as your captain
   In temptation's hour;
Let his will enfold you
   In its light and power.

4

Brothers, this Lord Jesus
   Shall return again,
With his Father's glory,
   With his angel train;
For all wreaths of empire
   Meet upon his brow,
And our hearts confess him
   King of glory now.

Caroline Maria Noel (1817–77)

It is a surprise to discover that the author of this powerful hymn was a frail Victorian lady, an invalid for the greater part of her life.

Miss Caroline Noel published it in 1870 for use on Ascension Day. It is based on a famous Bible passage (Philippians 2: 5–11) in which St Paul, in urging his readers to cultivate a humble spirit, points to the supreme example of Jesus who for our salvation became man and died on the cross. 'But God highly exalted him, and gave him the name which is above every name, that at the name of Jesus every knee should bow.'

11 *Be still, my soul*

Be still, my soul: the Lord is on thy side;
  Bear patiently the cross of grief or pain;
Leave to thy God to order and provide;
  In every change he faithful will remain.
Be still, my soul: thy best, thy heavenly Friend
Through thorny ways leads to a joyful end.

2

Be still, my soul: thy God doth undertake
  To guide the future as he has the past.
Thy hope, thy confidence let nothing shake;
  All now mysterious shall be bright at last.
Be still, my soul: the waves and winds still know
His voice who ruled them while he dwelt below.

3

Be still, my soul: when dearest friends depart,
  And all is darkened in the vale of tears,
Then shalt thou better know his love, his heart,
  Who comes to soothe thy sorrow and thy fears.
Be still, my soul: thy Jesus can repay,
From his own fullness, all he takes away.

4

Be still, my soul: the hour is hastening on
  When we shall be forever with the Lord,
When disappointment, grief, and fear are gone,
  Sorrow forgot, love's purest joys restored.
Be still, my soul: when change and tears are past,
All safe and blessèd we shall meet at last.

Tr. Jane Laurie Borthwick (1813–97)

Miss Jane Borthwick, a Scotswoman, made English translations of many German hymns. This one was published as long ago as 1855.

It was largely forgotten until some unknown musician had the idea of setting it to the chorale-like melody from the symphonic poem *Finlandia* by Sibelius. Words and music perfectly matched, and in this form the hymn soon became popular.

The original hymn was entitled 'Submission'—a theme that runs through all the stanzas.

12 Be thou my Vision

Be thou my Vision, O Lord of my heart,
Be all else but naught to me, save that thou art;
Be thou my best thought in the day and the night,
Both waking and sleeping, thy presence my light.

2

Be thou my Wisdom, be thou my true Word;
Be thou ever with me, and I with thee, Lord;
Be thou my great Father, and I thy true son;
Be thou in me dwelling, and I with thee one.

3

Be thou my Breastplate, my sword for the fight;
Be thou my whole armour, be thou my true might;
Be thou my soul's shelter, be thou my strong tower,
O raise thou me heavenward, great Power of my
    power.

4

Riches I heed not, nor man's empty praise,
Be thou mine inheritance now and always;
Be thou and thou only the first in my heart;
O Sovereign of heaven, my treasure thou art.

5

High King of heaven, thou heaven's bright Sun,
O grant me its joys, after victory is won;
Great Heart of my own heart, whatever befall,
Still be thou my Vision, O Ruler of all.

Tr. Mary Elizabeth Byrne (1881–1931)
Versified by Eleanor H. Hull (1860–1935)

We owe this thoroughly Irish hymn to two scholarly Irish women. In 1905 Miss Mary Byrne, an acknowledged expert in her nation's ancient language, made a prose translation in English of a poem dating from about the eighth century.

A few years later Dr Eleanor Hull turned the prose into poetry and published it in her *Poem Book of the Gael*, 1912. The result is our hymn: a prayer for such a vision of God that he may be our all-in-all throughout life's journey.

The attractive tune *Slane*, to which the words are sung, is a traditional Irish air.

13 *Blessed assurance, Jesus is mine*

Blessed assurance, Jesus is mine:
O what a foretaste of glory divine!
Heir of salvation, purchase of God;
Born of his Spirit, washed in his blood:

This is my story, this is my song,
Praising my Saviour all the day long.

2

Perfect submission, perfect delight,
Visions of rapture burst on my sight;
Angels descending bring from above
Echoes of mercy, whispers of love:

3

Perfect submission, all is at rest,
I in my Saviour am happy and blest—
Watching and waiting, looking above,
Filled with his goodness, lost in his love:

Frances Jane van Alstyne (Fanny Crosby) (1820–1915)

The American Mrs Van Alstyne—better known by her maiden name of Fanny Crosby—was blind almost from birth. Nevertheless, she wrote an enormous number of hymns and songs, many of which became extremely popular in the last century in connection with the Moody and Sankey missions. Some, like the present one, have now taken on a new lease of life as a result of the Billy Graham crusades around the world.

'Blessed assurance' is a good type of gospel song and one of Fanny Crosby's best. But it would hardly have survived all these years without the rousing tune which Mrs Phoebe Knapp (another American lady) wrote for it in 1875.

See also no. 95.

14 *Breathe on me, Breath of God*

Breathe on me, Breath of God,
Fill me with life anew,
That I may love what thou dost love,
And do what thou wouldst do.

2

Breathe on me, Breath of God,
Until my heart is pure,
Until with thee I will one will,
To do and to endure.

3

Breathe on me, Breath of God,
Blend all my soul with thine,
Until this earthly part of me
Glows with the fire divine.

4

Breathe on me, Breath of God,
So shall I never die,
But live with thee the perfect life
Of thine eternity.

Edwin Hatch (1835–89)

Not many popular hymns have been written by learned professors of theology. This one is an exception. Dr Edwin Hatch was an Oxford scholar who achieved international fame in the last century.

But there was another side to him. He was also a man of deep piety and childlike faith, as this hymn reveals. It is a prayer that the life-giving 'Breath of God' (the Holy Spirit) may cleanse and sanctify our inner life and set it aglow with divine love. (In Greek the word for *spirit* is the same as that for breath or wind.)

15 *Brightest and best of the sons of the morning*

Brightest and best of the sons of the morning,
  Dawn on our darkness, and lend us thine aid;
Star of the east, the horizon adorning,
  Guide where our infant Redeemer is laid.

2

Cold on his cradle the dew-drops are shining;
  Low lies his head with the beasts of the stall;
Angels adore him in slumber reclining,
  Maker and Monarch and Saviour of all.

3

Say, shall we yield him, in costly devotion,
    Odours of Edom, and offerings divine,
Gems of the mountain, and pearls of the ocean,
    Myrrh from the forest, or gold from the mine?

4

Vainly we offer each ample oblation,
    Vainly with gifts would his favour secure:
Richer by far is the heart's adoration,
    Dearer to God are the prayers of the poor.

Reginald Heber (1783–1826)

When Reginald Heber's Epiphany hymn was first published in 1811 some pious people took exception to it. They argued that the opening lines involved the worship of a star!

The hymn, of course, has nothing whatever to do with that. But it *is* very much concerned with the subject of worship and asks the question: How are we to worship God in a way acceptable to him?

The answer is that what he values most is not the sort of lavish gifts offered by the magi, but the adoration of the *heart*. The prayers of the poor are worth more to him than the treasures of the rich.

See also no. 35.

16 *Christ is the King! O friends rejoice*

Christ is the King! O friends rejoice;
Brothers and sisters, with one voice
Make all men know he is your choice.
Alleluia.

2

O magnify the Lord, and raise
Anthems of joy and holy praise
For Christ's brave saints of ancient days.
Alleluia.

3

They with a faith for ever new
Followed the King, and round him drew
Thousands of faithful men and true.
Alleluia.

4

O Christian women, Christian men,
All the world over, seek again
The Way disciples followed then.
Alleluia.

5

Christ through all ages is the same:
Place the same hope in his great name,
With the same faith his word proclaim.
Alleluia.

6

Let Love's unconquerable might
Your scattered companies unite
In service to the Lord of light.

Alleluia.

7

So shall God's will on earth be done,
New lamps be lit, new tasks begun,
And the whole Church at last be one.

Alleluia.

G. K. A. Bell (1883–1958)

George Bell, the author of this hymn, was Bishop of Chichester from 1929 to 1958, and became one of the outstanding leaders of the English Church in this century.

His passionate concern was for the unity of the Church—and of the churches—and this is reflected in his hymn. It calls upon all Christian men and women to hold fast to the faith of Christ's first disciples and follow in their steps, bound together by 'Love's unconquerable might'.

17 *Come down, O Love divine*

Come down, O Love divine,
Seek thou this soul of mine,
And visit it with thine own ardour glowing;
O Comforter, draw near,
Within my heart appear,
And kindle it, thy holy flame bestowing.

2

O let it freely burn,
Till earthly passions turn
To dust and ashes, in its heat consuming;
And let thy glorious light
Shine ever on my sight,
And clothe me round, the while my path illuming.

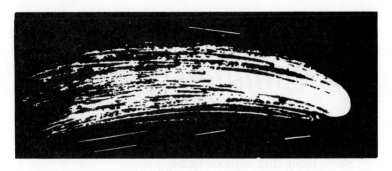

3

Let holy charity
Mine outward vesture be,
And lowliness become mine inner clothing;
　True lowliness of heart,
　Which takes the humbler part,
And o'er its own shortcomings weeps with loathing.

4

And so the yearning strong,
With which the soul will long,
Shall far outpass the power of human telling;
　For none can guess its grace,
　Till he become the place
Wherein the Holy Spirit makes his dwelling.

Bianco da Siena (d. 1434)
Tr. Richard Frederick Littledale (1833–90)

This hymn is a prayer to the Holy Spirit, who is addressed as 'Love divine'. How are
we to understand that title?

On the day of Pentecost the Spirit came on Christ's disciples in semblance of fire;
and love is like fire, warm, aflame, glowing. The hymn takes up this idea in its
opening verses. And since the Spirit is holy love, we go on to pray that he will clothe
us with the same character.

The popularity of this fifteenth-century Italian hymn is almost entirely due to the
haunting tune which Vaughan Williams specially composed for it. He named it
Down Ampney after the Gloucestershire village where he was born.

18 *Come, Holy Ghost, our souls inspire*

Come, Holy Ghost, our souls inspire,
And lighten with celestial fire;
Thou the anointing Spirit art,
Who dost thy sevenfold gifts impart:

2

Thy blessèd unction from above
Is comfort, life, and fire of love;
Enable with perpetual light
The dullness of our blinded sight:

3

Anoint and cheer our soilèd face
With the abundance of thy grace:
Keep far our foes, give peace at home;
Where thou art guide no ill can come.

4

Teach us to know the Father, Son,
And thee, of both, to be but One;
That through the ages all along
This may be our endless song:
   'Praise to thy eternal merit,
   Father, Son, and Holy Spirit.' Amen.

John Cosin (1594–1672)

Several English versions have been made of the ancient Latin hymn *Veni Creator Spiritus* which goes back at least to the ninth century.

This one, by John Cosin, Bishop of Durham from 1660 to 1672, is by far the best known. It was included in the Ordinal of the Book of Common Prayer, 1662, and is still regularly used at ordinations and on other solemn occasions.

The first two stanzas are a prayer to the Creator Spirit to inspire, enlighten, and sanctify our lives. In the final verse we pray that we may know God in the mystery of his being as Father, Son, and Holy Spirit; and the hymn ends with a doxology.

19 *Come, ye thankful people, come*

Come, ye thankful people, come,
Raise the song of harvest-home:
All is safely gathered in,
Ere the winter storms begin;
God, our Maker, doth provide
For our wants to be supplied:
Come to God's own temple, come,
Raise the song of harvest-home.

2

All this world is God's own field,
Fruit unto his praise to yield;
Wheat and tares together sown,
Unto joy or sorrow grown;
First the blade, and then the ear,
Then the full corn shall appear:
Lord of harvest, grant that we
Wholesome grain and pure may be.

3

For the Lord our God shall come,
And shall take his harvest home;
From his field shall in that day
All offences purge away;
Give his angels charge at last
In the fire the tares to cast;
But the fruitful ears to store
In his garner evermore.

4

Even so, Lord, quickly come
To thy final harvest-home:
Gather thou thy people in,
Free from sorrow, free from sin;
There, for ever purified,
In thy presence to abide:
Come, with all thine angels, come,
Raise the glorious harvest-home.

Henry Alford (1810–71)

This is probably the most popular of all harvest hymns. It was written by Henry Alford, Dean of Canterbury from 1857 to 1871.

He was a distinguished New Testament scholar, so it is not surprising that the hymn is broadly based on one of our Lord's parables, that of the wheat and the tares (Matthew 13: 24–30). This fact accounts for the note of judgement which is so prominent in the hymn.

Dean Alford was a man of broad sympathies and generous spirit. Throughout his ministry he maintained close relations with the Free Churches—something common enough now but all too rare in those days.

20 *Crown him with many crowns*

Crown him with many crowns,
The Lamb upon his throne;
Hark how the heavenly anthem drowns
All music but its own.
Awake, my soul, and sing
Of him who died for thee;
And hail him as thy matchless King
Through all eternity.

2

Crown him the Virgin's Son,
The God incarnate born,
Whose conquering arm those trophies won
Which now his brow adorn;
The Saviour long foretold,
The Branch of Jesse's stem,
The eternal Shepherd of his fold,
The Babe of Bethlehem.

3

Crown him the Lord of life,
Who triumphed o'er the grave,
And rose victorious in the strife
For those he came to save.
His glories now we sing
Who died and rose on high,
Who died eternal life to bring,
And lives that death may die.

4

Crown him the Lord of heaven,
    Enthroned in worlds above,
The King of kings to whom is given
    The wondrous name of Love.
    Hail him the Prince of peace,
    Whose power a sceptre sways
From pole to pole, that wars may cease,
    And all be love and praise.

5

Crown him the Lord of years,
    The Potentate of time,
Creator of the rolling spheres,
    Ineffably sublime:
    All hail, Redeemer, hail!
    For thou hast died for me:
Thy praise shall never, never fail
    Throughout eternity.

Matthew Bridges (1800–94)
Godfrey Thring (1823–1903)

In his vision of Christ in the glory of heaven, St John noted that 'on his head were many crowns' (Revelation 19: 12). It was those words that inspired the writing of this hymn.

Matthew Bridges composed it at the age of 48, shortly after entering the Roman Catholic Church. Some thirty years later it was altered and added to by Godfrey Thring, a prebendary of Wells Cathedral. This explains why slightly different versions of the hymn are to be found.

In whatever form we sing it, we are celebrating the kingship of Christ—what the Puritans delighted to call 'the crown rights of the Redeemer'.

21 Dear Lord and Father of mankind

Dear Lord and Father of mankind,
　Forgive our foolish ways;
Re-clothe us in our rightful mind,
In purer lives thy service find,
　In deeper reverence praise.

2

In simple trust like theirs who heard,
　Beside the Syrian sea,
The gracious calling of the Lord,
Let us, like them, without a word
　Rise up and follow thee.

3

O Sabbath rest by Galilee,
  O calm of hills above,
Where Jesus knelt to share with thee
The silence of eternity,
  Interpreted by love!

4

Drop thy still dews of quietness,
  Till all our strivings cease;
Take from our souls the strain and stress,
And let our ordered lives confess
  The beauty of thy peace.

5

Breathe through the heats of our desire
  Thy coolness and thy balm;
Let sense be dumb, let flesh retire;
Speak through the earthquake, wind, and fire,
  O still small voice of calm!

John Greenleaf Whittier (1807–92)

John Greenleaf Whittier, the American poet, was a Quaker. As such he was not accustomed to singing hymns in worship, and he disclaimed being a hymn-writer because he knew nothing of music.

Nevertheless, several of his poems have found their way into our hymnals and none has become more popular than this.

In this hymn Whittier emphasizes the Quaker ideals of simplicity, stillness, silence, and insists that the essence of religion consists not in outward forms but in quiet, spiritual communion with God.

See also no. 62.

22 *Eternal Father, strong to save*

Eternal Father, strong to save,
Whose arm hath bound the restless wave,
Who bidd'st the mighty ocean deep
Its own appointed limits keep;
O hear us when we cry to thee
For those in peril on the sea.

2

O Christ, whose voice the waters heard,
And hushed their raging at thy word,
Who walkedst on the foaming deep,
And calm amid the storm didst sleep;
O hear us when we cry to thee
For those in peril on the sea.

3

O Holy Spirit, who didst brood
Upon the waters dark and rude,
And bid their angry tumult cease,
And give, for wild confusion, peace;
O hear us when we cry to thee
For those in peril on the sea.

4

O Trinity of love and power,
Our brethren shield in danger's hour;
From rock and tempest, fire and foe,
Protect them wheresoe'er they go;
    Thus evermore shall rise to thee
    Glad hymns of praise from land and sea.

William Whiting (1825–78)

The sailors' hymn, as it is universally known, was written by William Whiting, a master at Winchester College Choristers' School, for a pupil who was about to sail for America.

He entitled it 'For those at sea' and added the text: 'These men see the works of the Lord, and his wonders in the deep' (Psalm 107: 24).

The verses follow the familiar Trinitarian pattern and are full of biblical allusions. The hymn first appeared in *Hymns Ancient and Modern*, 1861, set to the renowned tune *Melita* composed for it by Dr J. B. Dykes. Words and music have remained securely wedded ever since.

23 *Father, hear the prayer we offer*

Father, hear the prayer we offer;
  Not for ease that prayer shall be,
But for strength that we may ever
  Live our lives courageously.

2

Not for ever in green pastures
  Do we ask our way to be;
But the steep and rugged pathway
  May we tread rejoicingly.

3

Not for ever by still waters
Would we idly rest and stay;
But would smite the living fountains
From the rocks along our way.

4

Be our strength in hours of weakness,
In our wanderings be our guide;
Through endeavour, failure, danger,
Father, be thou at our side.

Love Maria Willis (1824–1908)

Mrs Maria Willis, the author of this hymn, was the wife of a New York doctor. She wrote it in 1859 as a poem for a religious magazine. A few years later it was revised and published in an American hymn-book.

The hymn may be regarded as a complement to the words of Psalm 23 about the Lord leading us in green pastures and beside still waters. It paints the other side of the picture. Life is often a 'steep and rugged pathway' and the hymn is a prayer that we may be given courage to tread it 'rejoicingly' with the Lord at our side.

24 *Fight the good fight with all thy might*

Fight the good fight with all thy might;
Christ is thy strength, and Christ thy right;
Lay hold on life, and it shall be
Thy joy and crown eternally.

2

Run the straight race through God's good grace,
Lift up thine eyes and seek his face;
Life with its way before thee lies,
Christ is the path, and Christ the prize.

3

Cast care aside, lean on thy Guide;
His boundless mercy will provide;
Trust, and thy trusting soul shall prove
Christ is its life and Christ its love.

4

Faint not nor fear, his arms are near;
He changeth not, and thou art dear;
Only believe, and thou shalt see
That Christ is all in all to thee.

John Samuel Bewley Monsell (1811–75)

From its opening words this hymn appears to be a Christian battle song. But that is not so. After the first two lines it has nothing more to say about the good fight or any other kind of fight.

But it does have a lot to say about faith—and about Christ; and this is what gives the hymn its distinctive character.

Note the strong imperatives that punctuate the stanzas: Lay hold on life! Run the straight race! Cast care aside! Faint not nor fear! Only believe!

The author, John Samuel Monsell, was an Irish parson who came to England in 1853 and was later rector of St Nicholas, Guildford. He died there as the result of a tragic accident while inspecting reconstruction work on his church.

See also no. 73.

25 *For all the saints*

For all the saints who from their labours rest,
Who thee by faith before the world confessed,
Thy name, O Jesu, be for ever blest:
    Alleluia!

2

Thou wast their rock, their fortress, and their might;
Thou, Lord, their captain in the well-fought fight;
Thou in the darkness drear their one true light:
    Alleluia!

3

O may thy soldiers, faithful, true, and bold,
Fight as the saints who nobly fought of old,
And win with them the victor's crown of gold:
    Alleluia!

4

O blest communion, fellowship divine!
We feebly struggle, they in glory shine;
Yet all are one in thee, for all are thine:
    Alleluia!

5

And when the strife is fierce, the warfare long,
Steals on the ear the distant triumph-song,
And hearts are brave again, and arms are strong:
    Alleluia!

6

The golden evening brightens in the west;
Soon, soon to faithful warriors cometh rest;
Sweet is the calm of Paradise the blest:
> Alleluia!

7

But lo, there breaks a yet more glorious day;
The saints triumphant rise in bright array:
The King of glory passes on his way:
> Alleluia!

8

From earth's wide bounds, from ocean's farthest coast,
Through gates of pearl streams in the countless host,
Singing to Father, Son, and Holy Ghost:
> Alleluia!

William Walsham How (1823–97)

This is certainly the most popular of all hymns for the feast of All Saints
(1 November). And rightly so, for it has about it the inspirational and imaginative
touch required of a hymn on the Church Triumphant and the Communion of Saints.

Its popularity in modern times has been increased by the splendid tune *Sine
Nomine* ('without a name') composed for it by Vaughan Williams for the *English
Hymnal*, 1906.

The hymn was written by William Walsham How, one of the leading English
hymn-writers in the last century. After 26 years of obscurity as a country parson he
became suffragan bishop for the East End of London. There he was greatly loved by
the poor, and especially the children. He was later Bishop of Wakefield.

26 Give me joy in my heart

Give me joy in my heart, keep me praising,
 Give me joy in my heart, I pray;
Give me joy in my heart, keep me praising,
 Keep me praising till the break of day.

Sing hosanna, sing hosanna,
Sing hosanna to the King of kings!
Sing hosanna, sing hosanna,
Sing hosanna to the King!

2
Give me peace in my heart, keep me loving . . .

3
Give me love in my heart, keep me serving . . .

Traditional

This cheerful song belongs to the class of 'pop hymns', as they have been called.
Both words and music are traditional; their origin is unknown.
 Almost certainly the song was written for children. It is a great favourite with them
as well as with adults who love to join in. And why not? The infectious melody sets
everybody singing 'hosanna to the King of kings'.

27 *Glorious things of thee are spoken*

Glorious things of thee are spoken,
  Zion, city of our God!
He whose word cannot be broken
  Formed thee for his own abode:
On the Rock of Ages founded,
  What can shake thy sure repose?
With salvation's walls surrounded,
  Thou may'st smile at all thy foes.

2

See, the streams of living waters,
  Springing from eternal love,
Well supply thy sons and daughters,
  And all fear of want remove.
Who can faint while such a river
  Ever flows their thirst to assuage—
Grace which, like the Lord the giver,
  Never fails from age to age.

3

Saviour, if of Zion's city
    I, through grace, a member am,
Let the world deride or pity,
    I will glory in thy name:
Fading is the worldling's pleasure,
    All his boasted pomp and show;
Solid joys and lasting treasure
    None but Zion's children know.

John Newton (1725–1807)

John Newton, the author of 'Amazing grace' (no. 7) and 'How sweet the name of
Jesus sounds' (no. 36), wrote this splendid hymn about the Church and headed it
'Zion, or the City of God'.

Zion is the poetic name for Jerusalem: the city beloved of God, chosen and
founded by him and sanctified by his presence. It is therefore a fitting symbol of the
Church, the true Zion, securely built on the Rock of ages and constantly replenished
by 'streams of living water'.

All this is wonderful. But the greatest wonder, as the final verse affirms, is that we
ourselves are citizens of this glorious Zion—all by God's grace.

28 *God moves in a mysterious way*

God moves in a mysterious way
   His wonders to perform;
He plants his footsteps in the sea,
   And rides upon the storm.

2

Deep in unfathomable mines
   Of never-failing skill
He treasures up his bright designs,
   And works his sovereign will.

3

Ye fearful saints, fresh courage take;
   The clouds ye so much dread
Are big with mercy, and shall break
   In blessings on your head.

4

Judge not the Lord by feeble sense
But trust him for his grace;
Behind a frowning providence
He hides a smiling face.

5

Blind unbelief is sure to err,
And scan his work in vain;
God is his own interpreter,
And he will make it plain.

William Cowper (1731–1800)

Written by the poet William Cowper, this is certainly the greatest hymn on the subject of divine providence—that is, the ways of God in his dealings with mankind.

What a difficult subject! Yes, for God's ways are often 'mysterious', beyond our comprehension, as Cowper recognizes in his opening line.

This is something we must accept. But that doesn't mean that life is all mystery or that God is inactive.

If you look carefully at the hymn you will find two contrasting ideas running through it. On the one hand, perplexity in the face of life's baffling and inexplicable happenings. On the other, confidence in God's wise and merciful ordering of our lives as he works his sovereign will.

29 Great is thy faithfulness, O God my Father

Great is thy faithfulness, O God my Father,
  There is no shadow of turning with thee;
Thou changest not, thy compassions, they fail not;
  As thou hast been thou for ever wilt be:

  Great is thy faithfulness! Great is thy faithfulness!
  Morning by morning new mercies I see;
  All I have needed thy hand has provided.
  Great is thy faithfulness, Lord, unto me.

2

Summer and winter, and springtime and harvest,
  Sun, moon and stars in their courses above,
Join with all nature in manifold witness
  To thy great faithfulness, mercy and love:

3

Pardon for sin and a peace that endureth,
  Thy own dear presence to cheer and to guide;
Strength for today and bright hope for tomorrow,
  Blessings all mine, with ten thousand beside!

Thomas O. Chisholm (1866–1960)

That 'God is faithful' is one of the big, fundamental truths of the Bible. He can never break his word or change his purposes. He is always and utterly trustworthy.

Thomas Chisholm, an American Methodist minister, took this as the theme of his hymn, published in 1923. The tune was written for it by William Runyan, another Methodist minister, who died in 1957.

The three stanzas emphasize God's unchanging and unchangeable character; the constancy of the created order as a witness to this; and the assurance of God's pardon and presence among the countless blessings of his love.

30 *Guide me, O thou great Jehovah*

Guide me, O thou great Jehovah,
  Pilgrim through this barren land;
I am weak, but thou art mighty,
  Hold me with thy powerful hand;
    Bread of heaven,
Feed me till I want no more.

2

Open now the crystal fountain
  Whence the healing stream doth flow:
Let the fire and cloudy pillar
  Lead me all my journey through;
    Strong deliverer,
Be thou still my strength and shield.

3

When I tread the verge of Jordan,
  Bid my anxious fears subside;
Death of death, and hell's destruction,
  Land me safe on Canaan's side;
    Songs and praises
I will ever give to thee.

William Williams (1716–91)

How much a hymn's popularity depends on its tune! This famous Welsh hymn was written well over 200 years ago by William Williams, known as 'the sweet singer of Wales' and one of its great preachers.

However, the tune *Cwm Rhondda* to which we now sing the words is comparatively modern. It was composed by John Hughes (1873–1932) for a Welsh song festival in 1905 and at once became immensely popular the world over.

As for the words, the hymn is a pilgrim's prayer based on the Bible story of the Israelites' journey through the wilderness to the promised land. This is taken as a picture of our Christian path in life until at last we cross the river of death and land safe in heaven.

31 *Hail the day that sees him rise*

Hail the day that sees him rise,
To his throne above the skies;
Christ, awhile to mortals given,
Enters now the highest heaven:
                    Alleluia!

2

There for him high triumph waits:
Lift your heads, eternal gates;
Christ hath conquered death and sin;
Take the King of glory in:
                    Alleluia!

3

Lo, the heaven its Lord receives,
Yet he loves the earth he leaves;
Though returning to his throne,
Still he calls mankind his own:
                    Alleluia!

4

See, he lifts his hands above;
See, he shows the prints of love;
Hark, his gracious lips bestow
Blessings on his Church below:
                    Alleluia!

5

Still for us he intercedes,
His prevailing death he pleads,
Near himself prepares our place,
He the first-fruits of our race:
                        Alleluia!

6

Lord, though parted from our sight,
Far above the starry height,
Grant our hearts may thither rise,
Seeking thee above the skies:
                        Alleluia!

Charles Wesley (1707–88)

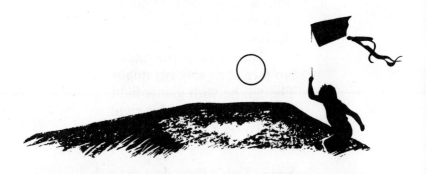

Charles was the younger brother of the more illustrious John Wesley, the leader of the Methodist movement in the eighteenth century. Both men were ordained ministers of the Church of England and devout churchmen.

Theirs was a marvellous partnership. If John was pre-eminently the organizer and preacher, Charles was the unrivalled poet whose hymns poured out in an unending stream for the Methodist people to sing.

Some of the best known are those he wrote for the great Christian festivals. This is his hymn for Ascensiontide. And what a magnificent hymn it is—a joyful celebration of Christ's completed work on earth and of his triumphal entry into heaven.

For other hymns by Wesley see nos. 8, 40, 49, 55, 64, 71.

32 *He who would valiant be*

He who would valiant be
'Gainst all disaster,
Let him in constancy
    Follow the Master.
There's no discouragement
Shall make him once relent
His first avowed intent
    To be a pilgrim.

2

Who so beset him round
With dismal stories,
Do but themselves confound—
    His strength the more is.
No foes shall stay his might,
Though he with giants fight:
He will make good his right
    To be a pilgrim.

3

Since, Lord, thou dost defend
Us with thy Spirit,
We know we at the end
    Shall life inherit.
Then fancies flee away!
I'll fear not what men say,
I'll labour night and day
    To be a pilgrim.

Percy Dearmer (1867–1936) after John Bunyan (1628–88)

John Bunyan was not a hymn-writer, nor was he much of a poet. But in his immortal allegory *Pilgrim's Progress* he occasionally introduces some simple verses to lighten the story.

The present hymn is an adaptation by Percy Dearmer of the pilgrim's song beginning 'Who would true valour see, let him come hither'. At this point in the allegory Bunyan invites the reader to 'come hither' and look at Mr Valiant-for-Truth and see in him an example of a courageous and faithful pilgrim.

The tune *Monk's Gate* to which we sing the hymn—whether in the original or this adapted version—was arranged by Vaughan Williams from an old Sussex folksong.

33 *Hills of the north, rejoice*

Hills of the north, rejoice;
　River and mountain-spring,
Hark to the advent voice;
　Valley and lowland, sing!
Though absent long, your Lord is nigh;
He judgement brings and victory.

2

Isles of the southern seas,
　Deep in your coral caves
Pent be each warring breeze,
　Lulled be your restless waves:
He comes to reign with boundless sway,
And makes your wastes his great highway.

3

Lands of the east, awake,
    Soon shall your sons be free;
The sleep of ages break,
    And rise to liberty.
On your far hills, long cold and grey,
Has dawned the everlasting day.

4

Shores of the utmost west,
    Ye that have waited long,
Unvisited, unblest,
    Break forth to swelling song;
High raise the note, that Jesus died,
Yet lives and reigns, the Crucified.

5

Shout, while ye journey home!
    Songs be in every mouth!
Lo, from the north we come,
    From east and west and south.
City of God, the bond are free,
We come to live and reign in thee!

Charles Edward Oakley (1832–65)

Charles Edward Oakley, the original author of this missionary hymn, was a highly
gifted man and a brilliant scholar. He might well have become one of the leading
English hymn-writers, but he died at the age of 33 while rector of St Paul's, Covent
Garden.

  This is the only hymn he left behind. It remained little known for nearly 50 years till
Martin Shaw composed for it the tune *Little Cornard* (the name of a Suffolk village)
and this at once made it popular.

34 *Holy God, we praise thy name*

Holy God, we praise thy name,
Lord of all, we bow before thee;
All on earth thy power proclaim,
All in heaven above adore thee,
Boundless is thy vast domain,
Everlasting is thy reign.

2

Hear the loud celestial hymn,
Angel choirs above are raising,
Cherubim and seraphim,
In unceasing chorus praising,
Fill the heavens with sweet accord:
Holy, holy, holy Lord.

3

Holy Father, holy Son,
Holy Spirit, three we name thee,
While in essence only one,
Undivided God we claim thee,
And adoring bend the knee,
While we own the mystery.

4

Spare thy people, Lord, we pray,
By a thousand snares surrounded;
Keep us free from sin today,
Never let us be confounded:
All my trust I place in thee,
Never, Lord, abandon me.

Clarence Alphonsus Walworth (1820–1900)
Adapted by Anthony G. Petti (1932–85)

This hymn is a free rendering of parts of the ancient Latin canticle *Te Deum laudamus* ('We praise thee, O God') which has been used in Christian worship since the fifth century. Anglicans are familiar with it because of its place in the morning service of the Book of Common Prayer.

The present metrical version dates from the middle of the last century. Its author, Clarence Walworth—an American by birth—was a Roman Catholic priest of the Redemptorist Order. His hymn, long popular in the United States, is now becoming widely known throughout the world.

35 *Holy, holy, holy, Lord God Almighty*

Holy, holy, holy, Lord God Almighty!
Early in the morning our song shall rise to thee:
Holy, holy, holy, merciful and mighty,
God in Three Persons, blessèd Trinity!

2

Holy, holy, holy! all the saints adore thee,
Casting down their golden crowns around the
glassy sea,
Cherubim and Seraphim falling down before thee,
Which wert, and art, and evermore shalt be.

3

Holy, holy, holy! though the darkness hide thee,
  Though the eye of sinful man thy glory may not
    see,
Only thou art holy; there is none beside thee,
  Perfect in power, in love, and purity.

4

Holy, holy, holy, Lord God Almighty!
  All thy works shall praise thy name in earth and
    sky and sea;
Holy, holy, holy, merciful and mighty,
  God in Three Persons, blessèd Trinity!

Reginald Heber (1783–1826)

At Oxford Reginald Heber won the Newdigate Prize for poetry. Soon after being
ordained he set about fulfilling his heart's ambition: to compile a new collection of
hymns of high poetical quality for the worship of the Church of England.

The task was never completed, owing to his early death in India as Bishop of
Calcutta. But many of his hymns have survived, the finest of them all being this one
for Trinity Sunday.

It is a majestic paraphrase of Revelation 4: 8–11, a passage in which we catch a
vision of God enthroned in heavenly majesty, surrounded by an angelic choir
endlessly chanting 'Holy, holy, holy is the Lord God Almighty, who was, and is, and
is to come'.

See also no. 15.

36 *How sweet the name of Jesus sounds*

How sweet the name of Jesus sounds
   In a believer's ear!
It soothes his sorrows, heals his wounds,
   And drives away his fear.

2

It makes the wounded spirit whole,
   And calms the troubled breast;
'Tis manna to the hungry soul,
   And, to the weary, rest.

3

Dear name! the rock on which I build,
   My shield and hiding-place,
My never-failing treasury filled
   With boundless stores of grace.

4

Jesus, my shepherd, brother, friend,
   My prophet, priest, and king,
My lord, my life, my way, my end,
   Accept the praise I bring.

5

Weak is the effort of my heart,
    And cold my warmest thought;
But when I see thee as thou art,
    I'll praise thee as I ought.

6

Till then I would thy love proclaim
    With every fleeting breath;
And may the music of thy name
    Refresh my soul in death.

John Newton (1725–1807)

There was a time in John Newton's past when he had lived a godless life and blasphemed the name of Jesus. But by God's 'amazing grace' (see no. 7) the blasphemer had become a believer, as this hymn makes plain.

Many hymns have been written about the name of Jesus. Newton's approach to the theme is characteristic of the man. He begins by extolling the Saviour's name in purely general terms (verses 1 and 2); but he is not content with that. He cannot think of Jesus in a detached manner. So the remaining verses become personal as he testifies to what Jesus means to him.

See also no. 27.

37 *I heard the voice of Jesus say*

I heard the voice of Jesus say,
  'Come unto me and rest;
Lay down, thou weary one, lay down
  Thy head upon my breast.'
I came to Jesus as I was,
  Weary, and worn, and sad;
I found in him a resting-place,
  And he has made me glad.

2

I heard the voice of Jesus say,
  'Behold, I freely give
The living water, thirsty one:
  Stoop down, and drink, and live.'
I came to Jesus, and I drank
  Of that life-giving stream;
My thirst was quenched, my soul revived,
  And now I live in him.

3

I heard the voice of Jesus say,
  'I am this dark world's light:
Look unto me, thy morn shall rise,
  And all thy day be bright.'
I looked to Jesus, and I found
  In him my star, my sun;
And in that light of life I'll walk
  Till travelling days are done.

Horatius Bonar (1808–89)

Dr Horatius Bonar has been called the prince of Scottish hymn-writers. He was a man of immense gifts and tireless energy and in his day he built up a big reputation as preacher, scholar, and author. But it is by his hymns—and he wrote many of them, apparently as a sort of spare-time hobby—that he is now remembered.

The present is one of his earliest. It was written for the children of his Sunday school at Kelso, where he served his first charge, and was entitled 'the Voice from Galilee'. The voice of course is that of Jesus, the voice of invitation heard in the first half of each verse. In the second half we raise *our* voice in grateful response to his call.

38 *Immortal, invisible, God only wise*

Immortal, invisible, God only wise,
In light inaccessible hid from our eyes,
Most blessèd, most glorious, the Ancient of Days,
Almighty, victorious, thy great name we praise.

2

Unresting, unhasting, and silent as light,
Nor wanting, nor wasting, thou rulest in might;
Thy justice like mountains high soaring above
Thy clouds which are fountains of goodness and love.

3

To all life thou givest, to both great and small;
In all life thou livest, the true life of all;
We blossom and flourish as leaves on the tree,
And wither and perish; but naught changeth thee.

4

Great Father of glory, pure Father of light,
Thine angels adore thee, all veiling their sight;
All laud we would render: O help us to see
'Tis only the splendour of light hideth thee.

Walter Chalmers Smith (1824–1908)

Walter Chalmers Smith was a Scotsman. Born in Aberdeen and educated at the city's grammar school and university, he became one of the leading scholars and preachers of the Free Church of Scotland.

He found relief from the burden of his labours—so he explained—in writing poetry. Of his many hymns this is by far the best known. It is a hymn of praise to God as Creator, based on the words of 1 Timothy 1: 17 (AV): 'Now unto the King eternal, immortal, invisible, the only wise God, be honour and glory for ever and ever.'

Its popular tune *St Denio* is a Welsh hymn melody.

39 *In heavenly love abiding*

In heavenly love abiding,
　No change my heart shall fear;
And safe is such confiding,
　For nothing changes here:
The storm may roar without me,
　My heart may low be laid;
But God is round about me,
　And can I be dismayed?

2

Wherever he may guide me,
　No want shall turn me back;
My Shepherd is beside me,
　And nothing can I lack:
His wisdom ever waketh,
　His sight is never dim;
He knows the way he taketh,
　And I will walk with him.

3

Green pastures are before me,
  Which yet I have not seen;
Bright skies will soon be o'er me,
  Where darkest clouds have been;
My hope I cannot measure,
  My path to life is free;
My Saviour has my treasure,
  And he will walk with me.

Anna Laetitia Waring (1823–1910)

Anna Waring was a Welsh woman. Born in Glamorganshire, she grew up as a Quaker but later became an Anglican. Later still she moved to Bristol, where she was an assiduous prison visitor. She had a keen intellect and taught herself Hebrew so that she could read the Psalms daily in their original tongue.

Of the forty or so hymns she wrote this is the best known. It is based on Psalm 23, particularly verse 4: 'Yea, though I walk through the valley of the shadow of death I will fear no evil, for thou art with me.' All through the hymn runs a note of serene confidence in the Lord's unfailing presence and guardian care.

40 Jesu, lover of my soul

Jesu, lover of my soul,
 Let me to thy bosom fly,
While the nearer waters roll,
 While the tempest still is high:
Hide me, O my Saviour, hide,
 Till the storm of life is past;
Safe into the haven guide,
 O receive my soul at last.

2

Other refuge have I none;
 Hangs my helpless soul on thee;
Leave, ah, leave me not alone,
 Still support and comfort me.
All my trust on thee is stayed,
 All my help from thee I bring;
Cover my defenceless head
 With the shadow of thy wing.

3

Plenteous grace with thee is found,
 Grace to cover all my sin;
Let the healing streams abound;
 Make and keep me pure within.
Thou of life the fountain art;
 Freely let me take of thee;
Spring thou up within my heart,
 Rise to all eternity.

Charles Wesley (1707–88)

This was once the best known of all Charles Wesley's hymns. Though not so popular today, it still retains its strong spiritual appeal.

Nothing is known of how he came to write it. The romantic stories that used to be told about its origin (e.g. that a bird in a storm took shelter in Wesley's breast) are purely legendary and must be forgotten.

The title Wesley gave the hymn was 'In temptation' and this is the key to its meaning. It is a prayer to be used amid life's testings and troubles, symbolized by the wild tempestuous sea. At such times the believer flies to Christ for refuge and prays,

> Hide me, O my Saviour, hide,
> Till the storm of life is past.

41 *Jesus, good above all other*

Jesus, good above all other,
Gentle child of gentle mother,
In a stable born our brother,
  Give us grace to persevere.

2

Jesus, cradled in a manger,
For us facing every danger,
Living as a homeless stranger,
  Make we thee our King most dear.

3

Jesus, for thy people dying,
Risen Master, death defying,
Lord in heaven, thy grace supplying,
  Keep us to thy presence near.

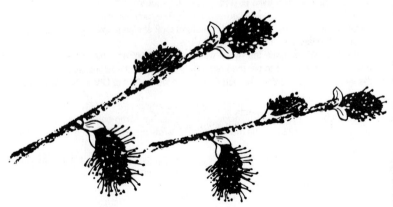

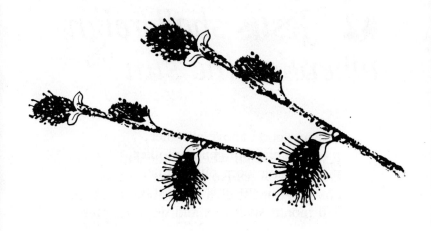

4

Jesus, who our sorrows bearest,
All our thoughts and hopes thou sharest;
Thou to man the truth declarest;
    Help us all thy truth to hear.

5

Lord, in all our doings guide us;
Pride and hate shall ne'er divide us;
We'll go on with thee beside us,
    And with joy we'll persevere!

Percy Dearmer (1867–1936)

Canon Percy Dearmer was a great hymn lover and knew a lot about hymns. Among his many accomplishments he edited the once famous hymn-book *Songs of Praise*, first published in 1925. Of the many hymns he wrote none is now better known than this.

Intended to be used by children, it unfolds in a simple way the story of Jesus' earthly life and his sympathy with human need. It concludes, as it begins, with a prayer to persevere.

42 *Jesus shall reign where'er the sun*

Jesus shall reign where'er the sun
Doth his successive journeys run;
His kingdom stretch from shore to shore,
Till moons shall wax and wane no more.

2

People and realms of every tongue
Dwell on his love with sweetest song,
And infant voices shall proclaim
Their early blessings on his name.

3

Blessings abound where'er he reigns;
The prisoner leaps to lose his chains;
The weary find eternal rest,
And all the sons of want are blest.

4

Let every creature rise and bring
Peculiar honours to our King;
Angels descend with songs again,
And earth repeat the long amen.

Isaac Watts (1674–1748)

Dr Isaac Watts is rightly known as the father of English hymnody. Until his time, congregational singing in church and chapel was confined to the old metrical psalms, most of them of poor literary quality.

It is to Watts's lasting credit that as a young man preparing to be a Dissenting minister he broke with this tradition and began writing hymns suitable for Christian worship. Others soon followed his example.

This hymn is a free paraphrase of part of Psalm 72, which speaks of an ideal king whose reign of righteousness would extend throughout the world. Watts boldly identifies that king. '*Jesus* shall reign' he begins, and with glances at the psalm proceeds to build up a glowing picture of Christ's universal kingdom.

See also nos. 65 and 99.

43 *Just as I am, without one plea*

Just as I am, without one plea
But that thy blood was shed for me,
And that thou bidd'st me come to thee,
    O Lamb of God, I come.

2

Just as I am, though tossed about,
With many^a conflict, many^a doubt,
Fightings and fears within, without,
    O Lamb of God, I come.

3

Just as I am, poor, wretched, blind;
Sight, riches, healing of the mind,
Yea, all I need, in thee to find,
    O Lamb of God, I come.

4

Just as I am, thou wilt receive,
Wilt welcome, pardon, cleanse, relieve;
Because thy promise I believe,
    O Lamb of God, I come.

5

Just as I am (thy love unknown
Has broken every barrier down),
Now to be thine, yea, thine alone,
    O Lamb of God, I come.

Just as I am, of that free love
The breadth, length, depth, and height to prove,
Here for a season, then above,
    O Lamb of God, I come.

Charlotte Elliott (1789–1871)

Charlotte Elliott was a clergyman's daughter. In her early thirties she was living in her father's London vicarage when there came to stay the Swiss evangelist, Dr César Malan. Observing her restless and unhappy state, he asked her about her faith. Had she come to Jesus?

After some hesitation she admitted, 'I do want to come to him, but I don't know how to come.' 'Come to him just as you are,' he replied. She did so and found peace of heart.

The hymn was not written till twelve years later. She was then an invalid and living with her brother at Brighton. One afternoon, in a mood of doubt and despondency because of her poor health, she recalled Dr Malan's words and quite spontaneously the words of the hymn came into her mind.

44 *King of glory, King of peace*

King of glory, King of peace,
  I will love thee;
And, that love may never cease,
  I will move thee.
Thou hast granted my request,
  Thou hast heard me;
Thou didst note my working breast,
  Thou hast spared me.

2

Wherefore with my utmost art
  I will sing thee,
And the cream of all my heart
  I will bring thee.
Though my sins against me cried,
  Thou didst clear me,
And alone, when they replied,
  Thou didst hear me.

3

Seven whole days, not one in seven,
   I will praise thee;
In my heart, though not in heaven,
   I can raise thee.
Small it is, in this poor sort
   To enrol thee;
E'en eternity's too short
   To extol thee.

George Herbert (1593–1633)

George Herbert, the eighteenth-century poet-parson, belonged to a distinguished English family. In early life he served at the court of King James I. Later, disillusioned with the glamour of the court, he dedicated himself to the service of the King of kings and was ordained. His last three years were spent as rector of a Wiltshire village where he proved himself a model parish priest.

Many of his poems, published a year after his early death, have been turned into hymns, like the present one. He entitled it simply 'Praise'. It stresses that praise is the expression of our love for God, that it must occupy all of life ('seven whole days . . .'), and that it demands the best we have to offer ('the cream of all my heart').

45 *Lead, kindly light*

Lead, kindly light, amid the˄encircling gloom,
    Lead thou me on;
The night is dark, and I am far from home,
    Lead thou me on.
Keep thou my feet; I do not ask to see
The distant scene; one step enough for me.

2

I was not ever thus, nor prayed that thou
    Should'st lead me on;
I loved to choose and see my path; but now
    Lead thou me on.
I loved the garish day, and, spite of fears,
Pride ruled my will: remember not past years.

3

So long thy power hath blessed me, sure it still
    Will lead me on,
O'er moor and fen, o'er crag and torrent, till
    The night is gone;
And with the morn those angel faces smile,
Which I have loved long since, and lost awhile.

John Henry Newman (1801–90)

John Henry Newman wrote these verses at the age of 32 when vicar of St Mary's, Oxford. On returning from a holiday in Sicily his boat was becalmed for a week in the Straits of Bonifacio, and it was there, he said, that he wrote 'Lead, kindly light'.

At the time he was grappling with the deep religious questions which twelve years later led him to enter the Church of Rome. Not surprisingly, then, his poem (it was not intended to be a hymn) was a prayer for divine guidance.

'The night is dark', he confessed, and accordingly he addressed God as the kindly light. The phrase 'Lead thou me on'—repeated a number of times—is the essence of the prayer.

46 *Lead us, heavenly Father, lead us*

Lead us, heavenly Father, lead us
   O'er the world's tempestuous sea;
Guard us, guide us, keep us, feed us,
   For we have no help but thee;
Yet possessing every blessing
   If our God our Father be.

2

Saviour, breathe forgiveness o'er us;
   All our weakness thou dost know,
Thou didst tread this earth before us,
   Thou didst feel its keenest woe;
Lone and dreary, faint and weary,
   Through the desert thou didst go.

3

Spirit of our God, descending,
   Fill our hearts with heavenly joy,
Love with every passion blending,
   Pleasure that can never cloy:
Thus provided, pardoned, guided,
   Nothing can our peace destroy.

James Edmeston (1791–1867)

There are several points of interest about this hymn. For one thing its author, James Edmeston, was a layman and one of the leading London architects of his day.

For another, the hymn was originally written for children: the children of an East End orphanage in which Edmeston took a particular interest.

Again, as we should expect of the work of an architect, his hymn follows a clear plan. It is an invocation of the Trinity, the three verses being addressed in turn to God the Father, the Son, and the Holy Spirit.

47 *Let all mortal flesh keep silence*

Let all mortal flesh keep silence,
  And with fear and trembling stand;
Ponder nothing earthly-minded,
  For with blessing in his hand
Christ our God to earth descendeth,
  Our full homage to demand.

King of kings, yet born of Mary,
 As of old on earth he stood,
Lord of lords, in human vesture—
 In the body and the blood—
He will give to all the faithful
 His own self for heavenly food.

3

Rank on rank the host of heaven
 Spreads its vanguard on the way,
As the Light of light descendeth
 From the realms of endless day,
That the powers of hell may vanish
 As the darkness clears away.

4

At his feet the six-winged Seraph;
 Cherubim with sleepless eye,
Veil their faces to the Presence,
 As with ceaseless voice they cry,
'Alleluia, Alleluia,
 Alleluia, Lord most high'.

Liturgy of St James
Tr. Gerard Moultrie (1829–85)

The story of this hymn begins back in the fourth century. It is part of the liturgy
(communion service) of the Greek Orthodox Church which was used at that time by
the Church in Jerusalem.

A hundred or so years ago scholars translated the Greek text of the liturgy into
English, and the Reverend Gerard Moultrie wrote this hymn as a free paraphrase of
one of the prayers. It is a eucharistic hymn, beginning on the note of wonder and
ending on the note of praise.

The French carol melody *Picardy* to which we sing it probably dates from the
seventeenth century.

48 *Lift high the cross*

Lift high the cross, the love of Christ proclaim
Till all the world adore his sacred name.

2

Come, brethren, follow where our Captain trod,
Our King victorious, Christ the Son of God:

3

Led on their way by this triumphant sign,
The hosts of God in conquering ranks combine:

4

Each new-born soldier of the Crucified
Bears on his brow the seal of him who died:

5

This is the sign which Satan's legions fear
And angels veil their faces to revere:

6

O Lord, once lifted on the glorious tree,
As thou hast promised, draw men unto thee:

7

From farthest regions let them homage bring,
And on his cross adore their Saviour King:

Michael Robert Newbolt (1874–1956)
Based on George William Kitchin (1827–1912)
(Five verses omitted)

This stirring and challenging processional hymn dates from 1887. It was written by George Kitchin, Dean of Winchester, for a missionary festival in his cathedral.

Some years later Canon Michael Newbolt, an Oxford scholar, revised it and it was published in *Hymns Ancient and Modern*, 1916, set to the fine tune *Crucifer* (meaning cross-bearer) composed for it by Sir Sydney Nicholson.

The main emphasis of the hymn is on the cross as the sign of victory. Probably Dean Kitchin had in mind the words which the Roman emperor Constantine heard in his vision of the cross: *in hoc signo vinces*, 'by this sign you shall conquer'.

49 *Lo! he comes with clouds descending*

Lo! he comes with clouds descending,
Once for favoured sinners slain;
Thousand thousand saints attending
Swell the triumph of his train:
Alleluia!
Christ appears, in power to reign.

2

Every eye shall now behold him
Robed in dreadful majesty;
Those who set at naught and sold him,
Pierced and nailed him to the tree,
Deeply wailing,
Shall the true Messiah see.

3

Those dear tokens of his Passion
  Still his dazzling body bears;
Cause of endless exultation
  To his ransomed worshippers;
    With what rapture
    Gaze we on those glorious scars!

4

Yea, amen, let all adore thee,
  High on thine eternal throne;
Saviour, take the power and glory: ·
  Claim the kingdom for thine own:
    Alleluia!
    Thou shalt reign, and thou alone.

Charles Wesley (1707–88)

Wesley's great Advent hymn was suggested to him by some crude verses of John Cennick—one of the early Methodist preachers and chiefly remembered as the author of 'Children of the heavenly King'. But he had little to do with the writing of this hymn. It is virtually Wesley's own work from start to finish.

The hymn is a vision of Christ's second coming in majesty and judgement. The language is borrowed from the Book of Revelation, and from one passage in particular (1: 7 AV): 'Behold, he cometh with clouds, and every eye shall see him, and they also which pierced him; and all kindreds of the earth shall wail because of him. Even so, Amen.'

The language of Revelation is difficult. This is because it is largely picture-language—that is, symbolic, not literal—and must be interpreted accordingly. So must the language of Wesley's hymn.

50 *Lord, enthroned in heavenly splendour*

Lord, enthroned in heavenly splendour,
  First-begotten from the dead,
Thou alone, our strong defender,
  Liftest up thy people's head.
        Alleluia!
    Jesu, true and living Bread.

2

Here our humblest homage pay we;
  Here in loving reverence bow;
Here for faith's discernment pray we,
  Lest we fail to know thee now.
        Alleluia!
    Thou art here, we ask not how.

3

Though the lowliest form doth veil thee,
   As of old in Bethlehem,
Here as there thine angels hail thee,
   Branch and Flower of Jesse's stem.
     Alleluia!
   We in worship join with them.

4

Paschal Lamb, thine offering, finished
   Once for all when thou wast slain,
In its fullness undiminished
   Shall for evermore remain,
     Alleluia!
   Cleansing souls from every stain.

5

Life-imparting, heavenly Manna,
   Stricken Rock with streaming side,
Heaven and earth with loud hosanna
   Worship thee, the Lamb who died,
     Alleluia!
   Risen, ascended, glorified.

George Hugh Bourne (1840–1925)

George Hugh Bourne was a parson-schoolmaster. He wrote many hymns but is now remembered by this one alone. Nevertheless, to have written even one hymn which is still being sung nearly a century later is no mean achievement. It was published in 1889 and set to Sir George Martin's tune *St Helen* which quickly established its popularity.

   It is a communion hymn and as such has the merit of being objective—not subjective—in character. When we sing it our thoughts are fixed not on ourselves but on Christ, the Lord enthroned in heaven—'risen, ascended, glorified'. That surely is how it should be.

51 *Lord, for tomorrow and its needs*

Lord for tomorrow and its needs
   I do not pray:
Keep me, my God, from stain of sin,
   Just for today.

2

Let me both diligently work
   And duly pray;
Let me be kind in word and deed,
   Just for today.

3

Let me be slow to do my will,
   Prompt to obey;
Help me to mortify my flesh,
   Just for today.

4

Let me no wrong or idle word
   Unthinking say:
Give me a seal upon my lips,
   Just for today.

5

Let me in season, Lord, be grave,
   In season gay;
Let me be faithful to your will,
   Just for today.

Sister M. Xavier (1856–1917)

The refrain 'Just for today' is the keynote of this hymn, ascribed to Sister M. Xavier. She was Sybil F. Partridge, who as a young girl entered the convent of Nôtre Dame in Liverpool. The hymn was written soon afterwards, as she herself related:

One of the elderly sisters fell seriously ill, and though she longed to be released, the end was continually delayed. While her strength seemed swiftly ebbing it was necessary to keep up her courage for at least one day more. With these thoughts running through my mind, one night in 1876 while sitting by her bedside I wrote the poem.

A little later it was printed in a religious journal. Much later still Sir Richard Terry (1865–1938) composed a tune for the words and thus turned the young nun's poem into a hymn.

52 *Living Lord*

Lord Jesus Christ,
You have come to us,
You are one with us,
    Mary's Son;
Cleansing our souls from all their sin,
Pouring your love and goodness in;
Jesus, our love for you we sing,
    Living Lord.

2

Lord Jesus Christ,
Now and every day
Teach us how to pray,
    Son of God.
You have commanded us to do
This in remembrance, Lord, of you:
Into our lives your power breaks through,
    Living Lord.

3

Lord Jesus Christ,
You have come to us,
Born as one of us,
    Mary's Son.
Led out to die on Calvary,
Risen from death to set us free,
Loving Lord Jesus, help us see
    You are Lord.

4

Lord Jesus Christ,
I would come to you,
Live my life for you,
    Son of God.
All your commands I know are true,
Your many gifts will make me new,
Into my life your power breaks through,
    Living Lord.

Patrick Appleford (b. 1924)

Patrick Appleford is one of the best known of our modern hymn-writers. In 1961, with the help of others, he founded the Twentieth Century Church Light Music Group. Its aim was to provide modern-style music for church worship and encourage the writing of hymns in contemporary idiom.

This hymn has proved to be his most popular. He wrote it, together with the tune, during his curacy days in East London. It was intended to be a communion hymn, as the second verse makes clear. When this is omitted, as is sometimes done, the hymn has a wider use.

53 *Lord of all hopefulness*

Lord of all hopefulness, Lord of all joy,
Whose trust, ever childlike, no cares could destroy,
Be there at our waking, and give us, we pray,
Your bliss in our hearts, Lord, at the break of the
    day.

2

Lord of all eagerness, Lord of all faith,
Whose strong hands were skilled at the plane and
    the lathe,
Be there at our labours, and give us, we pray,
Your strength in our hearts, Lord, at the noon of
    the day.

3

Lord of all kindliness, Lord of all grace,
Your hands swift to welcome, your arms to embrace,
Be there at our homing, and give us, we pray,
Your love in our hearts, Lord, at the eve of the day.

4

Lord of all gentleness, Lord of all calm,
Whose voice is contentment, whose presence is
    balm,
Be there at our sleeping, and give us, we pray,
Your peace in our hearts, Lord, at the end of the
    day.

Jan Struther (1901–53)

Hymns and tunes, as we know, go together. Normally the hymn is written first and the tune composed later. In this case it was the other way round.

Dr Percy Dearmer, editor of the hymnal *Songs of Praise*, wanted a new set of words for the Irish melody *Slane*, associated with 'Be thou my vision' (no. 12). He asked Jan Struther (the pen-name of a popular writer of verse) to see what she could do. He was delighted with the result—'a lovely example of the fitting together of thought, words and music'. He entitled it 'All Day Hymn', for the four verses refer respectively to morning, noon, evening, and night.

54 *Lord of the Dance*

I danced in the morning
  when the world was begun,
And I danced in the moon
  and the stars and the sun,
And I came down from heaven
  and I danced on the earth;
At Bethlehem I had my birth.

> *'Dance then wherever you may be;*
> *I am the Lord of the Dance,' said he,*
> *'And I'll lead you all, wherever you may be,*
> *And I'll lead you all in the dance,' said he.*

2

I danced for the scribe
  and the pharisee,
But they would not dance
  and they wouldn't follow me;
I danced for the fishermen,
  for James and John;
They came with me
  and the dance went on:

3

I danced on the Sabbath
  and I cured the lame:
The holy people
  said it was a shame.
They whipped and they stripped
  and they hung me high,
And they left me there
  on a cross to die:

4

I danced on a Friday
    when the sky turned black;
It's hard to dance
    with the devil on your back.
They buried my body
    and they thought I'd gone;
But I am the dance
    and I still go on:

5

They cut me down
    and I leap up high;
I am the life
    that'll never, never die;
I'll live in you
    if you'll live in me:
I am the Lord
    of the Dance, said he:

Sydney Carter (b. 1915)

Sydney Carter's popular hymn employs an unusual imagery, the imagery of the dance. The basic idea (it is found in the Old Testament) is that dancing is an expression of joy. The hymn therefore represents Christ's great work of redemption as a glad, triumphant achievement, by virtue of which he, the Lord of the Dance, invites us all to share in the joy of his salvation.

The hymn's rhythmic melody is an adaptation of an American Shaker tune. The Shakers were members of a sect who believed that Christ's second coming was imminent and expressed this hope in exuberant dancing and singing.

55 *Love divine, all loves excelling*

Love divine, all loves excelling,
  Joy of heaven, to earth come down,
Fix in us thy humble dwelling,
  All thy faithful mercies crown.
Jesu, thou art all compassion,
  Pure unbounded love thou art;
Visit us with thy salvation,
  Enter every trembling heart.

2

Finish then thy new creation,
  Pure and sinless let us be;
Let us see thy great salvation,
  Perfectly restored in thee,
Changed from glory into glory,
  Till in heaven we take our place,
Till we cast our crowns before thee,
  Lost in wonder, love, and praise.

Charles Wesley (1707–88)

Hymns are sometimes inspired by strange circumstances. Wesley got the idea of writing this one from a popular song of the day, 'Fairest isle, all isles excelling'—part of a play by Dryden set to music by Purcell.

It was probably Purcell's haunting tune that first caught Wesley's attention. It at once provided the music and metre for his hymn. The theme that suggested itself was that of love—but *divine* love, not the pagan love of Dryden's lyric.

So the poet's imagination was kindled and as a result we have this exquisite hymn celebrating the all-excelling love of Christ, with the prayer that this love may enter deeply into our lives.

56 Make me a channel of your peace

Make me a channel of your peace.
Where there is hatred, let me bring your love;
Where there is injury, your pardon, Lord;
And where there's doubt, true faith in you:

O Master, grant that I may never seek
So much to be consoled as to console;
To be understood as to understand;
To be loved, as to love with all my soul.

2

Make me a channel of your peace.
Where there's despair in life, let me bring hope;
Where there is darkness, only light;
And where there's sadness, ever joy:

3

Make me a channel of your peace.
It is in pardoning that we are pardoned,
In giving to all men that we receive,
And in dying that we're born to eternal life.

Sebastian Temple
Based on a traditional prayer

This hymn is a versified form of the well-known prayer, traditionally ascribed to St Francis of Assisi, beginning 'Lord, make me an instrument of thy peace'. Modern scholars tell us that the ascription is not correct, and it seems that no one knows who wrote the prayer.

But even if it was not actually written by Francis, at least it reflects the humble and compassionate spirit of the great thirteenth-century saint. And in the present form it makes an excellent modern-style hymn.

57 Mine eyes have seen the glory

Mine eyes have seen the glory of the coming of the
    Lord,
He is trampling out the vintage where the grapes of
    wrath are stored;
He has loosed the fateful lightning of his terrible
    swift sword:
  His truth is marching on.

Glory, glory alleluia!
Glory, glory alleluia!
Glory, glory alleluia!
His truth is marching on.

2

He has sounded forth the trumpet that shall never
    call retreat;
He is sifting out the hearts of men before his
    judgement seat;
O be swift, my soul, to answer him, be jubilant my
    feet!
    Our God is marching on.

3

In the beauty of the lilies Christ was born across the
    sea,
With a glory in his bosom that transfigures you and
    me;
As he died to make men holy, let us live to make
    men free,
    While God is marching on.

Julia Ward Howe (1819–1910)

This hymn is closely connected with the American Civil War and the abolition of slavery. Mrs Julia Ward Howe, a well-known poet and an ardent abolitionist, wrote it in 1861 shortly after the outbreak of the war.

At the time she was in Washington attending a review of Union troops and heard them singing 'John Brown's body'. Someone suggested to her that such a stirring tune deserved better and more permanent words. She accepted the challenge and wrote the hymn that same night.

Known as the Battle Hymn of the Republic it has achieved worldwide fame. It was sung at Sir Winston Churchill's funeral in St Paul's Cathedral, 30 January 1965.

58 *Morning has broken*

Morning has broken
  Like the first morning;
Blackbird has spoken
  Like the first bird.
    Praise for the singing!
    Praise for the morning!
    Praise for them, springing
    Fresh from the Word.

2

Sweet the rain's new fall,
  Sunlit from heaven,
Like the first dewfall
  On the first grass.
    Praise for the sweetness
    Of the wet garden,
    Sprung in completeness
    Where his feet pass.

3

Mine is the sunlight!
  Mine is the morning;
Born of the one light
  Eden saw play.
    Praise with elation!
    Praise ev'ry morning
    God's recreation
    Of the new day.

Eleanor Farjeon (1881–1965)

Doubtless much of the charm of this hymn lies in its Gaelic tune, *Bunessan*. The melody was noted down a century or so ago from the singing of a wandering highlander. However, it was not used as a hymn-tune till 1917 when it was set to Mary Macdonald's carol 'Child in the manger' and named after her birthplace in the Isle of Mull.

The present hymn was written by Miss Eleanor Farjeon to provide alternative words to fit the tune for the hymnal *Songs of Praise*, 1931. The theme suggested to her was thanksgiving for each new day. 'Morning has broken' was the happy outcome and continues to be very popular.

59 *My song is love unknown*

My song is love unknown,
  My Saviour's love to me,
Love to the loveless shown,
  That they might lovely be.
    O who am I,
      That for my sake
      My Lord should take
    Frail flesh and die?

2

He came from his blest throne,
  Salvation to bestow:
But men made strange, and none
  The longed-for Christ would know.
    But O, my friend,
      My friend indeed,
      Who at my need
    His life did spend!

3

Sometimes they strew his way,
  And his sweet praises sing;
Resounding all the day
  Hosannas to their King.
    Then 'Crucify!'
      Is all their breath,
      And for his death
    They thirst and cry.

4

In life, no house, no home
  My Lord on earth might have;
In death, no friendly tomb
  But what a stranger gave.
    What may I say?
      Heaven was his home:
      But mine the tomb
    Wherein he lay.

5

Here might I stay and sing,
  No story so divine;
Never was love, dear King,
  Never was grief like thine!
    This is my friend,
      In whose sweet praise
      I all my days
    Could gladly spend.

Samuel Crossman (1624–84)

Samuel Crossman, the author of this lovely lyric, became Dean of Bristol in 1684 and died shortly afterwards. This means that it was written over three hundred years ago (in fact in 1664); yet it was virtually lost sight of until the beginning of this century when it suddenly became widely known in the form of a hymn.

How did that happen? It is a familiar story. A new tune was provided for the words by John Ireland, a foremost English composer and song-writer. The tune *Love Unknown* (written, he said, in just fifteen minutes) almost at once popularized the hymn. It not only perfectly matches the seventeenth-century words but has the effect of heightening their meaning.

60 Now thank we all our God

Now thank we all our God,
With heart and hands and voices,
    Who wondrous things hath done,
In whom his world rejoices;
    Who from our mother's arms
        Hath blessed us on our way
    With countless gifts of love,
        And still is ours to-day.

2

O may this bounteous God
Through all our life be near us,
    With ever joyful hearts
And blessèd peace to cheer us;
    And keep us in his grace,
        And guide us when perplexed,
    And free us from all ills,
        In this world and the next.

3

All praise and thanks to God
The Father now be given,
  The Son, and him who reigns
With them in highest heaven;
  The one eternal God,
    Whom earth and heaven adore;
For thus it was, is now,
  And shall be evermore. Amen.

Martin Rinkart (1586–1649)
Tr. Catherine Winkworth (1827–78)

This great German hymn of thanksgiving is unlikely ever to grow old. Yet it was written over three centuries ago during the tragic period of the Thirty Years War. Its author Martin Rinkart, a Lutheran pastor, was deeply involved in the suffering of those years; but it seems that the war had no direct bearing on the hymn.

Rinkart, a great lover of music, wrote the first two verses as a 'grace' to be sung at meals in his own household. The first of them gratefully recognizes God's past goodness and mercy. The second is an act of prayer and seeks his guidance and help for the future. The third, a Trinitarian doxology, was not added until later.

61 Now the day is over

Now the day is over,
   Night is drawing nigh,
Shadows of the evening
   Steal across the sky.

2

Jesus, give the weary
   Calm and sweet repose;
With thy tenderest blessing
   May mine eyelids close.

3

Grant to little children
   Visions bright of thee;
Guard the sailors tossing
   On the deep blue sea.

4

Comfort every sufferer
 Watching late in pain;
Those who plan some evil
 From their sin restrain.

5

When the morning wakens,
 Then may I arise
Pure and fresh and sinless
 In thy holy eyes.

6

Glory to the Father,
 Glory to the Son,
And to thee, blest Spirit,
 Whilst all ages run. Amen.

Sabine Baring-Gould (1834–1924)

Sabine Baring-Gould had the reputation of being the most prolific author of his time. He published over 150 books on a wide variety of subjects. Now his fame rests almost entirely on his hymns. These include 'Onward, Christian soldiers' (no. 74) and 'Through the night of doubt and sorrow'.

  The present verses were written as an evening hymn for the children of his Sunday school at Horbury Bridge, Yorkshire. Its charm lies in its utter simplicity, and this is matched by the tune *Eudoxia* which the author composed for it.

62 *O brother man, fold to thy heart thy brother*

O brother man, fold to thy heart thy brother!
  Where pity dwells, the peace of God is there;
To worship rightly is to love each other,
  Each smile a hymn, each kindly deed a prayer.

2

For he whom Jesus loved hath truly spoken:
  The holier worship which he deigns to bless
Restores the lost, and binds the spirit broken,
  And feeds the widow and the fatherless.

3

Follow with reverent steps the great example
    Of him whose holy work was doing good;
So shall the wide earth seem our Father's temple,
    Each loving life a psalm of gratitude.

4

Then shall all shackles fall; the stormy clangour
    Of wild war-music o'er the earth shall cease;
Love shall tread out the baleful fire of anger,
    And in its ashes plant the tree of peace.

John Greenleaf Whittier (1807–92)

The American Quaker poet John Greenleaf Whittier is best known to hymn-lovers as the author of 'Dear Lord and Father of mankind' (no. 21). His Quaker faith, so evident in that hymn, also finds expression here. The verses reflect his social concern, his love for his fellows, and his interpretation of religion in terms of service, not services.

The lines are taken from a long poem he wrote in 1848 entitled 'Worship'. He headed it with the text of James 1:27: 'Pure religion before God the Father is this, to visit the fatherless and widows in their affliction, and to keep oneself unspotted from the world.'

Of the hymn's many tunes the most popular is certainly the *Londonderry Air.*

63 *O come, O come, Emmanuel*

O come, O come, Emmanuel,
And ransom captive Israel,
That mourns in lonely exile here,
Until the Son of God appear.
Rejoice, rejoice! Emmanuel
Shall come to thee, O Israel.

2

O come, O come, thou Lord of might,
Who to thy tribes, on Sinai's height,
In ancient times didst give the law
In cloud and majesty and awe:

3

O come, thou Rod of Jesse, free
Thine own from Satan's tyranny;
From depths of hell thy people save,
And give them victory o'er the grave:

4

O come, thou Dayspring, come and cheer
Our spirits by thine advent here;
Disperse the gloomy clouds of night,
And death's dark shadows put to flight:

5

O come, thou Key of David, come
And open wide our heavenly home;
Make safe the way that leads on high,
And close the path to misery:

Tr. John Mason Neale (1818–66)

What a splendid tune! But what obscure words! That is a likely first reaction to this famous Advent hymn. It has a long history, the details of which need not concern us. In brief, it is a translation of a medieval Latin hymn expressing an intense longing for the coming of Christ, who is addressed by various Old Testament titles such as the Rod of Jesse, the Dayspring, and the Key of David.

Our English version we owe to that prince of translators, Dr John Mason Neale. The tune *Veni Emmanuel* is of fifteenth-century origin and came from a service book used by French Franciscan nuns.

64 *O for a thousand tongues to sing*

O for a thousand tongues to sing
  My dear Redeemer's praise,
The glories of my God and King,
  The triumphs of his grace!

2

Jesus, the name that charms our fears,
  That bids our sorrows cease;
'Tis music in the sinner's ears,
  'Tis life and health and peace.

3

He speaks: and, listening to his voice
   New life the dead receive,
The mournful broken hearts rejoice,
   The humble poor believe.

4

Hear him, ye deaf; his praise, ye dumb,
   Your loosened tongues employ;
Ye blind, behold your Saviour come;
   And leap, ye lame, for joy!

5

My gracious Master and my God,
   Assist me to proclaim
And spread through all the earth abroad
   The honours of thy name.

Charles Wesley (1707–88)

Charles Wesley never forgot the day (Whit Sunday 1738) when there took place in his life the spiritual change he called his conversion (see no. 8). He was approaching the first anniversary of the day, when his friend Peter Böhler remarked to him, 'If I had a thousand tongues I would praise Christ with them all!'

The words set the poet's heart aglow, and to celebrate the anniversary he wrote this hymn in which with a full and thankful heart he tells of what Christ has done for him.

It was his conversion that turned Charles Wesley into a poet. Before that experience, though over 30 years of age, he had written no hymns. Afterwards he never stopped writing them until his death fifty years later.

65 *O God, our help in ages past*

O God, our help in ages past,
  Our hope for years to come,
Our shelter from the stormy blast,
  And our eternal home;

2

Under the shadow of thy throne
  Thy saints have dwelt secure;
Sufficient is thine arm alone,
  And our defence is sure.

3

Before the hills in order stood,
  Or earth received her frame,
From everlasting thou art God,
  To endless years the same.

4

A thousand ages in thy sight
  Are like an evening gone,
Short as the watch that ends the night
  Before the rising sun.

5

Time, like an ever-rolling stream,
  Bears all its sons away;
They fly forgotten, as a dream
  Dies at the opening day.

6

O God, our help in ages past,
  Our hope for years to come,
Be thou our guard while troubles last,
  And our eternal home.

Isaac Watts (1674–1748)

Dr Benjamin Jowett, Master of Balliol College Oxford, once asked a group of dons to jot down a list of the finest English hymns. The result was surprising. Each of the lists contained only one hymn and in every case it was the same: 'O God, our help in ages past'.

Here unquestionably is a really great English hymn and one of our national treasures. Written by Isaac Watts, it is a free paraphrase of the first part of Psalm 90, which begins (AV): 'Lord, thou hast been our dwelling place in all generations'. Watts gave his hymn a title: 'Man frail and God eternal'. This is the dominant note of the psalm, as also of the hymn.

See also nos. 42 and 99.

66 *O Jesus, I have promised*

O Jesus, I have promised
  To serve thee to the end;
Be thou for ever near me,
  My Master and my Friend;
I shall not fear the battle
  If thou art by my side,
Nor wander from the pathway
  If thou wilt be my guide.

2

O let me feel thee near me:
  The world is ever near;
I see the sights that dazzle,
  The tempting sounds I hear;
My foes are ever near me,
  Around me and within;
But, Jesus, draw thou nearer,
  And shield my soul from sin.

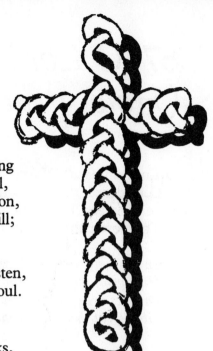

3

O let me hear thee speaking
  In accents clear and still,
Above the storms of passion,
  The murmurs of self-will;
O speak to reassure me,
  To hasten or control;
O speak, and make me listen,
  Thou guardian of my soul.

4

O let me see thy footmarks,
  And in them plant mine own;
My hope to follow duly
  Is in thy strength alone;
O guide me, call me, draw me,
  Uphold me to the end;
And then in heaven receive me,
  My Saviour and my Friend.

John Ernest Bode (1816–74)

This is often regarded as a confirmation hymn, and rightly so. John Bode wrote it for the confirmation of his own children when he was vicar of Castle Camps, Cambridgeshire. He was a scholarly man and something of a poet, yet of all his religious verse this hymn alone has stood the test of time.

It is a good hymn and has one distinct advantage. In spite of its original purpose it makes no specific mention of confirmation. This frees it from any denominational ties and gives it a wider appeal. Well over a century after it was written (about 1866) it is used in churches of all communions as a prayer of dedication to Christ's service.

67 *O Lord my God (How great thou art)*

O Lord my God! When I in awesome wonder
    Consider all the works thy hand hath made,
I see the stars, I hear the mighty thunder,
    Thy power throughout the universe displayed;

Then sings my soul, my Saviour God, to thee,
    How great thou art! How great thou art!
Then sings my soul, my Saviour God, to thee,
    How great thou art! How great thou art!

2

When through the woods and forest glades I wander,
    And hear the birds sing sweetly in the trees;
When I look down from lofty mountain grandeur,
    And hear the brook, and feel the gentle breeze;

3

And when I think that God His Son not sparing,
  Left Him to die—I scarce can take it in.
That on the cross my burden gladly bearing,
  He bled and died to take away my sin:

4

When Christ shall come with shout of acclamation
  And take me home—what joy shall fill my heart!
Then shall I bow in humble adoration
  And there proclaim, my God, how great thou art!

Tr. Stuart K. Hine (b. 1899)

Few would recognize this hymn from its first line, but the refrain at once identifies it:
'How great thou art!'
  Quite a long story lies behind it. The original version was written in Sweden in
about 1885 by Carl Boberg, a Christian minister who set it to a Swedish folk melody.
A German translation was made in 1907, followed a few years later by a Russian
one. This came to the notice of an English missionary working in the Ukraine, Stuart
Hine, who in turn produced our English version.
  The hymn is now being sung all round the world through the Billy Graham
crusades.

68 *O Love that wilt not let me go*

O Love that wilt not let me go,
   I rest my weary soul in thee:
I give thee back the life I owe,
That in thine ocean depths its flow
     May richer, fuller be.

2

O Light that followest all my way,
   I yield my flickering torch to thee:
My heart restores its borrowed ray,
That in thy sunshine's blaze its day
     May brighter, fairer be.

3

O Joy that seekest me through pain,
   I cannot close my heart to thee:
I trace the rainbow through the rain,
And feel the promise is not vain,
     That morn shall tearless be.

4

O Cross that liftest up my head,
   I dare not ask to fly from thee:
I lay in dust life's glory dead,
And from the ground there blossoms red
     Life that shall endless be.

George Matheson (1842–1906)

There is no truth in the story that George Matheson, a Scotsman, wrote this hymn after the girl he hoped to marry jilted him because he was going blind. He did indeed lose his sight before he was 20, but the hymn was not written till much later, when he was minister of Innellan.

The words came to him, he said, by a sudden inspiration. 'Something had happened, known only to myself, which caused me the most severe mental distress. The hymn was the fruit of that suffering.'

Here is the key to the meaning of the hymn with its difficult, mystical language. Suffering is the theme that runs through all four stanzas—suffering, and the love of God.

69 *O praise ye the Lord*

O praise ye the Lord! praise him in the height;
Rejoice in his word, ye angels of light;
Ye heavens, adore him, by whom ye were made,
And worship before him, in brightness arrayed.

2

O praise ye the Lord! praise him upon earth,
In tuneful accord, ye sons of new birth;
Praise him who hath brought you his grace from
    above,
Praise him who hath taught you to sing of his love.

3

O praise ye the Lord! thanksgiving and song
To him be outpoured all ages along:
For love in creation, for heaven restored,
For grace of salvation, O praise ye the Lord!

Henry Williams Baker (1821–77)

The fame of the Reverend Sir Henry Baker rests principally not on the hymns he wrote but on the hymn-book he created and to which he devoted most of his life. This was *Hymns Ancient and Modern*, first published in 1861. The book was an enormous success and immediately made hymn-singing popular in the Church of England.

    Of the many hymns he himself wrote, the best known is 'The King of love my shepherd is' (no. 87), a rendering of Psalm 23. 'O praise ye the Lord' is based on Psalm 150, a great psalm of praise. The hymn splendidly echoes its spirit and rings with praise from start to finish.

70 *O sacred head, sore wounded*

O sacred head, sore wounded,
  Defiled and put to scorn;
O kingly head, surrounded
  With mocking crown of thorn:
What sorrow mars thy grandeur?
  Can death thy bloom deflower?
O countenance whose splendour
  The hosts of heaven adore!

2

In thy most bitter Passion
  My heart to share doth cry,
With thee for my salvation
  Upon the cross to die.
Ah, keep my heart thus movèd
  To stand thy cross beneath,
To mourn thee, well-belovèd,
  Yet thank thee for thy death.

3

My days are few, O fail not,
  With thine immortal power,
To hold me that I quail not
  In death's most fearful hour:
That I may fight befriended,
  And see in my last strife
To me thine arms extended
  Upon the cross of life.

Tr. Paul Gerhardt (1607–76)
Par. Robert Bridges (1844–1930)

The story of this Passion hymn takes us back to the Middle Ages. The original Latin poem was probably written in the fourteenth century. A German version of the words by Paul Gerhardt was published in 1656, and it is this that forms the basis of the various English translations.

It has been said that the hymn, in passing from Latin into German and thence into English, 'proclaims in these tongues with equal effect the dying love of our Saviour, and our boundless indebtedness to him'.

The famous chorale to which it is sung was used several times by J. S. Bach in his *St Matthew Passion*.

71 *O thou who camest from above*

O thou who camest from above,
  The pure celestial fire to impart,
Kindle a flame of sacred love
  On the mean altar of my heart.

2

There let it for thy glory burn
  With inextinguishable blaze,
And trembling to its source return
  In humble prayer and fervent praise.

3

Jesu, confirm my heart's desire
  To work and speak and think for thee;
Still let me guard the holy fire,
  And still stir up thy gift in me.

4

Ready for all thy perfect will,
  My acts of faith and love repeat,
Till death thy endless mercies seal,
  And make the sacrifice complete.

Charles Wesley (1707–88)

Wesley attached to this hymn a rather odd text from Leviticus 6: 13: 'The fire shall ever be burning upon the altar; it shall never go out.' The words refer to the Jewish burnt offering in which the entire sacrifice was consumed by fire and kept continually burning on the altar.

Wesley took this as a picture of the Christian's entire and unceasing devotion to God. 'Fire' is the keyword of the hymn. The 'flame of sacred love' is to burn constantly in the believer's heart until his death, which is his final sacrifice and completes all that he has to offer to God.

72 *O worship the King*

O worship the King, all glorious above;
O gratefully sing his power and his love:
Our shield and defender, the ancient of days,
Pavilioned in splendour, and girded with praise.

2

O tell of his might, O sing of his grace;
Whose robe is the light, whose canopy space;
His chariots of wrath the deep thunder-clouds form,
And dark is his path on the wings of the storm.

3

This earth, with its store of wonders untold,
Almighty, thy power hath founded of old;
Hath stablished it fast by a changeless decree,
And round it hath cast, like a mantle, the sea.

4

Thy bountiful care what tongue can recite?
It breathes in the air, it shines in the light;
It streams from the hills, it descends to the plain,
And sweetly distils in the dew and the rain.

5

Frail children of dust, and feeble as frail,
In thee do we trust, nor find thee to fail;
Thy mercies how tender, how firm to the end,
Our maker, defender, redeemer, and friend.

6

O measureless might, ineffable love,
While angels delight to hymn thee above,
Thy humbler creation, though feeble their lays,
With true adoration shall sing to thy praise.

Robert Grant (1779–1838)

All sorts of people, both high and low, have written our hymns. This one is the work
of Sir Robert Grant, a distinguished layman of Scottish descent. After an outstanding career in the law he was knighted in 1834 and appointed Governor of Bombay.

The hymn was written in 1833. It is a free rendering of Psalm 104 which begins, 'O
Lord my God, thou art very great! Thou art clothed with honour and majesty.' The
psalm as a whole celebrates God's work in creation, and the hymn does the same in
richly poetical language. It brings out one point the psalm does not mention, that he
who is 'measureless might' is also 'ineffable love'.

73 *O worship the Lord in the beauty of holiness*

O worship the Lord in the beauty of holiness,
  Bow down before him, his glory proclaim;
With gold of obedience, and incense of lowliness,
  Kneel and adore him, the Lord is his name.

2

Low at his feet lay thy burden of carefulness,
  High on his heart he will bear it for thee,
Comfort thy sorrows and answer thy prayerfulness,
  Guiding thy steps as may best for thee be.

3

Fear not to enter his courts in the slenderness
  Of the poor wealth thou would'st reckon as thine;
Truth in its beauty, and love in its tenderness,
  These are the offerings to lay on his shrine.

4

These, though we bring them in trembling and
    fearfulness,
  He will accept for the name that is dear;
Mornings of joy give for evenings of tearfulness,
  Trust for our trembling, and hope for our fear.

John Samuel Bewley Monsell (1811–75)

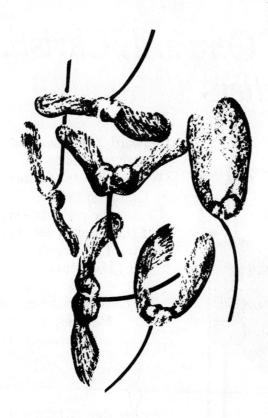

Another hymn by the author of 'Fight the good fight' (no. 24). Monsell wrote it for the Epiphany and therefore it has as its background the story of the wise men who came to Bethlehem seeking the new-born king. 'And they fell down and worshipped him, and offered him gifts . . .'

The hymn calls upon us to do something similar, for it is essentially a hymn about worship. But how are we to worship God? Not simply with our lips or in outward forms, but with adoring hearts and in holy, humble, and obedient lives. The language is poetical and mystical but by no means difficult to understand.

74 *Onward, Christian soldiers*

Onward, Christian soldiers,
    Marching as to war,
With the cross of Jesus
    Going on before!
Christ, the royal master,
    Leads against the foe;
Forward into battle,
    See! His banners go!

    Onward, Christian soldiers,
        Marching as to war,
    With the cross of Jesus
        Going on before!

2

At the sign of triumph
    Satan's host doth flee;
On then, Christian soldiers,
    On to victory!
Hell's foundations quiver
    At the shout of praise;
Brothers, lift your voices;
    Loud your anthems raise:

3

Crowns and thrones may perish,
　　Kingdoms rise and wane,
But the church of Jesus
　　Constant will remain;
Gates of hell can never
　　'Gainst that church prevail;
We have Christ's own promise,
　　And that cannot fail:

4

Onward, then, ye people!
　　Join our happy throng;
Blend with ours your voices
　　In the triumph-song:
Glory, laud, and honour
　　Unto Christ the King!
This through countless ages
　　Men and angels sing:

Sabine Baring-Gould (1834–1924)

In 1864 Sabine Baring-Gould was given charge of the mission church at Horbury Bridge in Yorkshire. He found that one of the big occasions was the Whit Monday procession when the children marched to an adjoining village, headed by a cross and banners, to share in a united festival. They were accustomed to sing while marching, and the new curate decided to write them a special hymn for the day.

The result was 'Onward, Christian soldiers'. It was afterwards printed in a church paper; but not much notice was taken of it till five years later, when Sir Arthur Sullivan wrote for it the celebrated tune *St Gertrude*. The hymn's popularity was then ensured once and for all.

See also no. 61.

75 *Our God reigns*

How lovely on the mountains are the feet of him
Who brings good news, good news,
Proclaiming peace, announcing news of happiness:
Your God reigns, your God reigns!

Our God reigns, our God reigns!
Our God reigns, our God reigns!

2

You watchmen lift your voices joyfully as one,
Shout for your King, your King.
See eye to eye the Lord restoring Zion:
Your God reigns, your God reigns!

3

Waste places of Jerusalem break forth with joy,
We are redeemed, we are redeemed.
The Lord has saved and comforted his people:
Your God reigns, your God reigns!

4

Ends of the earth, see the salvation of your God,
Jesus is Lord, is Lord.
Before the nations he has bared his holy arm:
Your God reigns, your God reigns!

Leonard E. Smith, Jnr. (b. 1942)

This popular song comes from America. Its author, Lenny Smith, wrote it in 1974 after passing through a period of spiritual depression. Hoping to find some comfort, he was reading his Bible and came to Isaiah 52: 7: 'How lovely on the mountains are the feet of him who brings good news, announcing peace, proclaiming news of happiness: your God reigns!'

Those words spoke directly to his heart. He saw that the gospel is the good news not only of God's love but of God's sovereignty, and that he is already reigning in the world. The hymn was the result of that revelation.

76 *Praise, my soul, the King of heaven*

Praise, my soul, the King of heaven;
  To his feet thy tribute bring.
Ransomed, healed, restored, forgiven,
  Who like thee his praise should sing?
    Praise him! Praise him!
  Praise the everlasting King!

2

Praise him for his grace and favour
  To our fathers in distress;
Praise him, still the same for ever,
  Slow to chide, and swift to bless.
    Praise him! Praise him!
  Glorious in his faithfulness.

3

Father-like, he tends and spares us;
  Well our feeble frame he knows;
In his hands he gently bears us,
  Rescues us from all our foes.
    Praise him! Praise him!
  Widely as his mercy flows.

4

Angels help us to adore him;
  Ye behold him face to face;
Sun and moon, bow down before him,
  Dwellers all in time and space.
    Praise him! Praise him!
  Praise with us the God of grace!

Henry Francis Lyte (1793–1847)

Henry Francis Lyte's fame used to rest almost entirely on 'Abide with me' (no. 1). But he is now probably better known as the author of this magnificent hymn of praise, which was chosen by Queen Elizabeth for her wedding to the Duke of Edinburgh, 20 November 1947.

Lyte published it in his collection of hymns *The Spirit of the Psalms*, 1834. As the title indicates, his purpose was not to provide a literal paraphrase of the psalms but rather to capture their underlying spirit and make them genuine acts of Christian worship.

This hymn is a superb example. It is a masterly rendering of Psalm 103 which begins 'Praise the Lord, O my soul!' It is assuredly a great hymn. It is also fine poetry and a reminder that in his student days at Dublin Lyte won the university's prize for an English poem three years in succession.

77 Praise to the Holiest in the height

Praise to the Holiest in the height,
  And in the depth be praise;
In all his words most wonderful,
  Most sure in all his ways.

2
O loving wisdom of our God!
  When all was sin and shame,
A second Adam to the fight
  And to the rescue came.

3
O wisest love! that flesh and blood,
  Which did in Adam fail,
Should strive afresh against the foe,
  Should strive and should prevail;

4
And that a higher gift than grace
  Should flesh and blood refine,
God's presence and his very self,
  And essence all-divine.

5

O generous love! that he who smote
   In Man, for man, the foe,
The double agony in Man,
   For man, should undergo;

6

And in the garden secretly,
   And on the cross on high,
Should teach his brethren, and inspire
   To suffer and to die.

7

Praise to the Holiest in the height,
   And in the depth be praise;
In all his words most wonderful,
   Most sure in all his ways.

John Henry Newman (1801–90)

The words of this hymn come from Newman's masterpiece, *The Dream of Gerontius*, 1865. The work traces the journey of a Christian soul (the aged monk Gerontius) from this world to the next through the gate of death. These verses are sung by an angelic choir as the soul enters paradise.

Newman never intended them to be a congregational hymn. Indeed, it is strange that they should have become so popular, for not only do they deal with the sombre subject of man's death but also contain some difficult theological language.

But, of course, the hymn is not only concerned with death. It is concerned far more with Christ's great redemption, his conquest of death. And that is what the complex language is all about.

78 *Praise to the Lord, the Almighty*

Praise to the Lord, the Almighty, the King of
 creation;
O my soul, praise him, for he is thy health and
 salvation:
    All ye who hear,
    Brothers and sisters, draw near,
Praise him in glad adoration.

2

Praise to the Lord, who o'er all things so
   wondrously reigneth,
Shelters thee under his wings, yea, so gently
   sustaineth:
            Hast thou not seen?
            All that is needful hath been
Granted in what he ordaineth.

3

Praise to the Lord, who doth prosper thy work and
   defend thee;
Surely his goodness and mercy here daily attend thee:
            Ponder anew
            What the Almighty can do,
Who with his love doth befriend thee.

4

Praise to the Lord, O let all that is in me adore him!
All that hath life and breath come now with praises
   before him!
            Let the amen
            Sound from his people again:
Gladly for aye we adore him!

Joachim Neander (1650–80)
Tr. Catherine Winkworth (1827–78)

We need not be surprised that so many of our hymns have a German origin. Hymn-singing as we know it today began in Germany at the Reformation, and more hymns have been written in German than in any other language.

This splendid hymn is an outpouring of praise to God as the creator, sovereign, and defender of his people. Its author, Joachim Neander, had spent a dissolute youth, but he was converted and became a Christian pastor. His ministry was very short, for he died of consumption at the age of 30. He left behind about sixty hymns, many of which are still sung in Germany.

See also no. 3.

79 *Rock of ages, cleft for me*

Rock of ages, cleft for me,
Let me hide myself in thee;
Let the water and the blood,
From thy riven side which flowed,
Be of sin the double cure:
Cleanse me from its guilt and power.

2

Not the labours of my hands
Can fulfil thy law's demands;
Could my zeal no respite know,
Could my tears for ever flow,
All for sin could not atone:
Thou must save, and thou alone.

3

Nothing in my hand I bring;
Simply to thy Cross I cling;
Naked, come to thee for dress;
Helpless, look to thee for grace;
Foul, I to the fountain fly;
Wash me, Saviour, or I die.

4

While I draw this fleeting breath,
When mine eyes are closed in death,
When I soar through tracts unknown,
See thee on thy judgement-throne;
Rock of ages, cleft for me,
Let me hide myself in thee.

Augustus Montague Toplady (1740–78)

We can forget the legend that Augustus Toplady, curate of Blagdon in Somerset, wrote this hymn while sheltering from a storm in the cleft of a rock in Burrington Combe. The hymn was written much later in his life and the legend did not circulate till seventy years after his death.

He drew the vivid imagery of the cleft rock from the Bible and other sources. Admittedly the hymn is open to criticism as a literary work, but there is no doubt about its spiritual appeal. In the best sense it is a gospel hymn with its unchanging message of the guilt of man, the grace of God, and the sufficiency of Christ.

80 *Seek ye first the kingdom of God*

Seek ye first the kingdom of God,
    And his righteousness,
And all these things shall be added unto you;
    Allelu-, Alleluia:

Alleluia, Alleluia, Alleluia,
Allelu-, Alleluia!

2

Ask, and it shall be given unto you;
    Seek, and ye shall find;
Knock, and the door shall be opened unto you;
    Allelu-, Alleluia:

3

Man shall not live by bread alone,
    But by every word
That proceeds from the mouth of the Lord;
    Allelu-, Alleluia:

Karen Lafferty (b. 1943)

This is an unusual hymn. The words are taken straight from the New Testament and are in fact the words of Jesus himself: words he spoke to his disciples long ago and still speaks to us today.

As it happens they all come from St Matthew's Gospel:

'Seek ye first the kingdom of God' (6: 33):

'Man shall not live by bread alone' (4: 4):

'Ask, and it shall be given unto you' (7: 7).

The words were selected and put together by Karen Lafferty, an American writer of gospel songs, who also composed the tune to accompany them. The Alleluias added at the end of each stanza impart to the hymn a needful note of praise.

81 *Spirit of God*

Spirit of God, in all that's true I know you;
Yours is the light that shines through thoughts and
   words.
Forgive my mind, slow as it is to read you,
My mouth so slow to speak the truth you are.

2

Spirit of God, in beauty I behold you;
Yours is the loveliness of all that's fair.
Forgive my heart, slow as it is to love you,
My soul so slow to wonder at your grace.

3

Spirit of God, in all that's good I meet you;
Yours is the rightness in each deed of love.
Forgive my will, slow as it is to serve you,
My feet so slow to go, my hands to do.

4

Spirit of God, in Jesus Christ you find me;
In Him you enter through the door of faith.
From deep within me take possession of me—
My will, my heart, my mind all matched to his.

Reginald T. Brooks (1918–85)

The author of this hymn, Reginald Thomas ('Peter') Brooks, was a Congregational minister. After serving churches in Skipton and Bradford he joined the Religious Broadcasting Department of the BBC, first in radio, later as a television producer. He wrote only a handful of hymns, but all are of high quality. 'Spirit of God' was his last.

The hymn was one of the prize-winning entries for the BBC's Songs of Praise Festival competition, 1985. As an invocation of the Holy Spirit—the Spirit of Truth, Beauty, Goodness, and of Christ—it is a fine piece of devotional writing, suitable for use in private prayer as much as in church worship.

82 *Stand up, stand up for Jesus*

Stand up, stand up for Jesus,
 Ye soldiers of the Cross!
Lift high his royal banner,
 It must not suffer loss.
From victory unto victory
 His army he shall lead,
Till every foe is vanquished,
 And Christ is Lord indeed.

2

Stand up, stand up for Jesus!
 The trumpet call obey;
Forth to the mighty conflict
 In this his glorious day.
Ye that are men, now serve him
 Against unnumbered foes;
Let courage rise with danger,
 And strength to strength oppose.

3

Stand up, stand up for Jesus!
 Stand in his strength alone;
The arm of flesh will fail you,
 Ye dare not trust your own.
Put on the gospel armour,
 Each piece put on with prayer;
When duty calls or danger,
 Be never wanting there!

4

Stand up, stand up for Jesus!
The strife will not be long;
This day the noise of battle,
The next the victor's song.
To him that overcometh,
A crown of life shall be;
He with the King of glory
Shall reign eternally.

George Duffield (1818–88)

A tragic story underlies this hymn. In 1858—the year of the great religious awakening in America—Dudley Tyng, a young Episcopal clergyman, was conducting a series of services for young men in Philadelphia.

But when the work was at its height he met with a terrible accident and died of his injuries a few days later. Asked on his deathbed if he had a message for the young men, he replied, 'Tell them to stand up for Jesus!'

His friend George Duffield, a Presbyterian minister, preached at the funeral. He told of the dying man's last message and then recited some verses he had written for the occasion. Those verses were our hymn—'Stand up for Jesus!' It was soon being sung all over America and in Britain.

83 *Tell out, my soul*

Tell out, my soul, the greatness of the Lord!
   Unnumbered blessings, give my spirit voice;
Tender to me the promise of his word;
   In God my Saviour shall my heart rejoice.

2

Tell out, my soul, the greatness of his Name!
   Make known his might, the deeds his arm has
     done;
His mercy sure, from age to age the same;
   His holy Name—the Lord, the Mighty One.

3

Tell out, my soul, the greatness of his might!
  Powers and dominions lay their glory by.
Proud hearts and stubborn wills are put to flight,
  The hungry fed, the humble lifted high.

4

Tell out, my soul, the glories of his word!
  Firm is his promise, and his mercy sure.
Tell out, my soul, the greatness of the Lord
  To children's children and for evermore!

Timothy Dudley-Smith (b. 1926)

This is undoubtedly the most widely known and frequently sung hymn written by a contemporary author. Since its publication in 1965 it has steadily found its way into every part of the world and into every modern hymnal.

It is a splendid poetical rendering of the song of Mary which we know as the *Magnificat* (Luke 1: 46–55). Bishop Dudley-Smith says he wrote it in 1961 on reading the version of the canticle in the New English Bible. He was struck by the opening words, 'Tell out, my soul, the greatness of the Lord!' and saw in them the first line of a poem. He speedily wrote the rest, based on the text of the NEB.

A few years later the poem became a hymn and has found an ideal partner in the tune *Woodlands*.

84 *The Church's one foundation*

The Church's one foundation
  Is Jesus Christ, her Lord;
She is his new creation
  By water and the word:
From heaven he came and sought her
  To be his holy bride,
With his own blood he bought her
  And for her life he died.

2

Elect from every nation
  Yet one o'er all the earth,
Her charter of salvation
  One Lord, one faith, one birth;
One holy name she blesses,
  Partakes one holy food,
And to one hope she presses
  With every grace endued.

3

Though with a scornful wonder
  Men see her sore oppressed,
By schisms rent asunder,
  By heresies distressed,
Yet saints their watch are keeping,
  Their cry goes up, 'How long?'
And soon the night of weeping
  Shall be the morn of song.

4

'Mid toil and tribulation,
 And tumult of her war,
She waits the consummation
 Of peace for evermore;
Till with the vision glorious
 Her longing eyes are blest,
And the great Church victorious
 Shall be the Church at rest.

5

Yet she on earth hath union
 With God the Three in One,
And mystic sweet communion
 With those whose rest is won:
O happy ones and holy!
 Lord, give us grace that we,
Like them, the meek and lowly,
 On high may dwell with thee.

Samuel John Stone (1839–1900)

The author of this hymn John Stone, a curate of Windsor, was a zealous High Churchman. Happily that fact has not limited the appeal or usefulness of his hymn. Christians of all types of churchmanship can cheerfully sing it and in doing so affirm the historic faith of the Church, which was John Stone's intention.

The hymn was written in a time of religious controversy and the young curate, then aged 27, considered it his duty to adopt the role of defender of the faith.

Never mind now the controversy, long since forgotten. Out of it emerged this powerful, confident hymn, certainly one of the great English hymns of the Victorian age.

85 *The day thou gavest*

The day thou gavest, Lord, is ended,
  The darkness falls at thy behest;
To thee our morning hymns ascended,
  Thy praise shall sanctify our rest.

2

We thank thee that thy Church unsleeping,
  While earth rolls onward into light,
Through all the world her watch is keeping,
  And rests not now by day or night.

3

As o'er each continent and island
  The dawn leads on another day,
The voice of prayer is never silent,
  Nor dies the strain of praise away.

4

The sun that bids us rest is waking
  Our brethren 'neath the western sky,
And hour by hour fresh lips are making
  Thy wondrous doings heard on high.

5

So be it, Lord! thy throne shall never,
  Like earth's proud empires, pass away;
Thy kingdom stands, and grows for ever,
  Till all thy creatures own thy sway.

John Ellerton (1826–93)

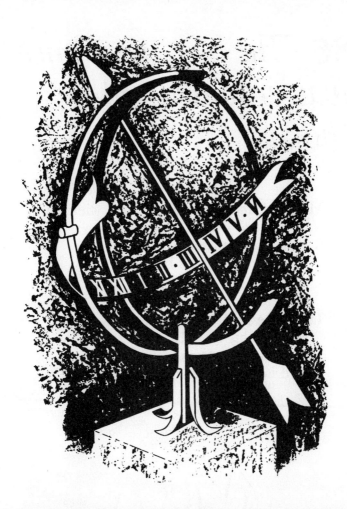

For many people this is the perfect evening hymn. It certainly makes a splendid finish to an evening service. But Canon John Ellerton, one of the leading Victorian hymnists, did not write it specifically for the evening hour. He published it in 1870 as part of an order of service for missionary meetings, and its missionary character is undeniable.

The hymn's dominant theme is the growing worldwide Church of Jesus Christ and its unbroken, unceasing offering of worship to God. The imagery of day and night, morning and evening, is used simply to demonstrate this. Few hymns so effectively give a congregation a sense of fellowship with other Christians around the world.

86 *The head that once was crowned with thorns*

The head that once was crowned with thorns
  Is crowned with glory now;
A royal diadem adorns
  The mighty victor's brow.

2

The highest place that heaven affords
  Is his, is his by right,
The King of kings and Lord of lords,
  And heaven's eternal Light;

3

The joy of all who dwell above,
   The joy of all below,
To whom he manifests his love,
   And grants his name to know.

4

To them the Cross with all its shame,
   With all its grace, is given;
Their name an everlasting name,
   Their joy the joy of heaven.

5

They suffer with their Lord below,
   They reign with him above;
Their profit and their joy to know
   The mystery of his love.

6

The Cross he bore is life and health,
   Though shame and death to him;
His people's hope, his people's wealth,
   Their everlasting theme.

Thomas Kelly (1769–1855)

The theme of this hymn by the Irish hymn-writer Thomas Kelly is the two coronations of Christ, the one on earth, the other in heaven.

Before his crucifixion the Roman soldiers placed on Jesus' head a crown of thorns and offered him mock homage as a king. Years later the apostle John was granted a vision of him in his heavenly majesty and saw that 'on his head were many crowns' (Revelation 19: 12).

Kelly links together these two crownings of Jesus, representing his shame and his glory. Moreover, he sees in this the pattern of our own Christian discipleship. Those who suffer with Christ will also reign with him.

87 *The King of love*

The King of love my Shepherd is,
  Whose goodness faileth never:
I nothing lack if I am his,
  And he is mine for ever.

2

Where streams of living waters flow
  My ransomed soul he leadeth;
And where the verdant pastures grow
  With food celestial feedeth.

3

Perverse and foolish oft I strayed;
    But yet in love he sought me,
And on his shoulder gently laid,
    And home, rejoicing, brought me.

4

In death's dark vale I fear no ill,
    With thee, dear Lord, beside me;
Thy rod and staff my comfort still,
    Thy Cross before to guide me.

5

Thou spread'st a table in my sight;
    Thy unction grace bestoweth;
And O, what transport of delight
    From thy pure chalice floweth!

6

And so through all the length of days
    Thy goodness faileth never:
Good Shepherd, may I sing thy praise
    Within thy house for ever.

Henry Williams Baker (1821–77)

The beautiful Shepherd Psalm (Psalm 23) has been a great favourite with the hymn-writers. There are several good metrical versions (see no. 88). Sir Henry Baker's approach to it is distinctive.

While borrowing the leading ideas of the psalm and some of its language, he treats it with a large amount of freedom and gives it a definitely Christian meaning.

The allusions to the Lord's table and the chalice (v. 5) invest it with a sacramental character. It is a perfect communion hymn.

When Sir Henry lay dying at the age of 55 he was heard quietly repeating to himself the verse 'Perverse and foolish oft I strayed . . .'.

88 *The Lord's my Shepherd*

The Lord's my Shepherd, I'll not want.
　He makes me down to lie
In pastures green: he leadeth me
　The quiet waters by.

2

My soul he doth restore again,
　And me to walk doth make
Within the paths of righteousness,
　E'en for his own name's sake.

3

Yea, though I walk in death's dark vale,
    Yet will I fear none ill:
For thou art with me, and thy rod
    And staff me comfort still.

4

My table thou hast furnishèd
    In presence of my foes;
My head thou dost with oil anoint,
    And my cup overflows.

5

Goodness and mercy all my life
    Shall surely follow me:
And in God's house for evermore
    My dwelling-place shall be.

Scottish Psalter (1650)

In a remarkable way the much loved twenty-third psalm suits all the vicissitudes of life and matches every mood of the human heart. The fact that it is sung frequently at both weddings and funerals is evidence of this.

Here we have the perfect metrical version, taken from the *Scottish Psalter* of 1650. Its authorship is unknown. It seems that several people had a hand in shaping its final form.

We are better placed when it comes to the tune *Crimond*, with which the hymn has been associated since Queen Elizabeth chose it for her marriage service in 1947. The melody was written by Miss Jessie Irvine (1836–87), whose father was for thirty years the minister at Crimond in Aberdeenshire.

89 *The old rugged cross*

On a hill far away stood an old rugged cross,
  The emblem of suffering and shame;
And I love that old cross where the dearest and best
  For a world of lost sinners was slain.

  So I'll cherish the old rugged cross
    Till my trophies at last I lay down;
  I will cling to the old rugged cross
    And exchange it some day for a crown.

2

Oh, the old rugged cross, so despised by the world,
  Has a wondrous attraction for me;
For the dear Lamb of God left his glory above
  To bear it to dark Calvary.

3

In the old rugged cross, stained with blood so
    divine,
  A wondrous beauty I see;
For 'twas on that old cross Jesus suffered and died
  To pardon and sanctify me.

4

To the old rugged cross I will ever be true,
  Its shame and reproach gladly bear;
Then he'll call me some day to my home far away.
  When his glory for ever I'll share.

George Bennard (1873–1958)

An all-time favourite gospel song in the United States, the land of its birth. George Bennard, a Methodist minister, wrote both words and music in 1913. He said that the inspiration was given him by God over a period of weeks following a mission he conducted in the small town of Albion, Michigan.

Bennard had formerly been a Salvation Army officer and this probably accounts for the character of the song and its haunting tune. It is difficult to explain the hymn's enormous popularity, but no doubt this has something to do with its message as well as with its melody.

90 *There is a green hill far away*

There is a green hill far away,
   Without a city wall,
Where the dear Lord was crucified,
   Who died to save us all.

2

We may not know, we cannot tell
   What pains he had to bear;
But we believe it was for us
   He hung and suffered there.

3

He died that we might be forgiven,
   He died to make us good;
That we might go at last to heaven,
   Saved by his precious blood.

4

There was no other good enough
   To pay the price of sin,
He only could unlock the gate
   Of heaven, and let us in.

5

O dearly, dearly has he loved,
   And we must love him too,
And trust in his redeeming blood,
   And try his works to do.

Cecil Frances Alexander (1818–95)

Another of Mrs Alexander's *Hymns for Little Children*, 1848, illustrating the articles
of the creed (see no. 5). This one is based on the words 'Suffered under Pontius
Pilate, was crucified, dead, and buried'. The opening lines may have been
suggested to her by the familiar sight of the massive city walls of Londonderry and
the green hills 'without'—that is, outside them.

   The purpose of the hymn is to answer the child's question, Why did Jesus die?
Mrs Alexander accomplishes the difficult task by the use of simple poetry and
picture language. Endless scholarly books have been written about the meaning of
the cross. This children's hymn tells us most of what we need to know and can
understand.

91 *Thine be the glory*

Thine be the glory, risen, conquering Son,
Endless is the victory thou o'er death hast won;
Angels in bright raiment rolled the stone away,
Kept the folded grave-clothes, where thy body lay.
   Thine be the glory, risen, conquering Son,
   Endless is the victory thou o'er death hast won.

2

Lo! Jesus meets us, risen from the tomb;
Lovingly he greets us, scatters fear and gloom;
Let the Church with gladness hymns of triumph
   sing,
For her Lord now liveth; death hath lost its sting.

3

No more we doubt thee, glorious Prince of Life;
Life is naught without thee: aid us in our strife;
Make us more than conquerors, through thy
  deathless love:
Bring us safe through Jordan to thy home above.

Edmond Budry (1854–1932)
Tr. Richard B. Hoyle (1875–1939)

This was originally a French hymn, *A toi la gloire*, by Edmond Budry, who for many years was pastor at Vevey, Switzerland. He wrote it in 1896 following the death of his first wife.

The English translation by Richard Hoyle, a Baptist minister and linguist, appeared in 1925. Since then it has become exceedingly popular in all parts of the world.

The words of the hymn, with their strong notes of joy and triumph, are largely derived from the Gospel narratives of the Lord's resurrection. As for the celebrated tune from Handel's *Judas Maccabaeus*, all one need say is that it is a worthy and perfect companion for the hymn.

92 *Thou whose almighty word*

Thou whose almighty word
Chaos and darkness heard
   And took their flight.
Hear us, we humbly pray,
And, where the gospel day
Sheds not its glorious ray,
   Let there be light.

2

Thou who didst come to bring,
On thy redeeming wing,
   Healing and sight,
Health to the sick in mind,
Sight to the inly blind,
O now to all mankind
   Let there be light.

3

Spirit of truth and love,
Life-giving, holy Dove,
  Speed forth thy flight;
Move o'er the waters' face,
Bearing the lamp of grace,
And in earth's darkest place
  Let there be light.

4

Blessèd and holy Three,
Glorious Trinity,
  Wisdom, Love, Might,
Boundless as ocean's tide
Rolling in fullest pride,
Through the world far and wide
  Let there be light.

John Marriott (1780–1825)

Like many another, this hymn probably owes its survival to its tune. *Moscow* was written by the Italian composer Felice de Giardini and later named after the city where he died.

The hymn's author, John Marriott, was a humble clergyman whose chief claim to fame was his friendship with Sir Walter Scott. Modestly he did not permit any of his hymns to be published in his lifetime. This one first gained publicity by being used at a missionary meeting shortly after his death.

It is essentially a missionary hymn and follows a clear Trinitarian pattern. The refrain 'Let there be light' is the first recorded utterance of God in the Bible.

93 *Through all the changing scenes of life*

Through all the changing scenes of life,
    In trouble and in joy,
The praises of my God shall still
    My heart and tongue employ.

2

O magnify the Lord with me,
    With me exalt his name;
When in distress to him I called,
    He to my rescue came.

3

The hosts of God encamp around
    The dwellings of the just;
Deliverance he affords to all
    Who on his succour trust.

4

O make but trial of his love;
  Experience will decide
How blest they are, and only they,
  Who in his truth confide.

5

Fear him, ye saints, and you will then
  Have nothing else to fear;
Make you his service your delight,
  Your wants shall be his care.

Nahum Tate (1652–1715) and Nicholas Brady (1659–1726)
in New Version (1696)

In 1696 the church people of England were given something of a shake-up by the publication of the New Version of the metrical psalms. They had long been accustomed to the old version (of Queen Elizabeth's time) and at first resented the new one.

It was the work of two Irish clergymen, Nahum Tate, the Poet Laureate (also the author of 'While shepherds watched') and Nicholas Brady, chaplain to King William. In the course of time their superior and more poetical version of the psalms won the book due recognition.

From it is derived this hymn, comprising a selection of stanzas from Psalm 34. It is a fairly free rendering of the psalm, but it is poetical as well as intelligible and the result is an excellent hymn of praise.

94 *Thy hand, O God, has guided*

Thy hand, O God, has guided
  Thy flock, from age to age;
The wondrous tale is written,
  Full clear, on every page;
Our fathers owned thy goodness,
  And we their deeds record;
And both of this bear witness,
  'One Church, one Faith, one Lord'.

2

Thy heralds brought glad tidings
  To greatest, as to least;
They bade men rise, and hasten
  To share the great King's feast;
And this was all their teaching,
  In every deed and word,
To all alike proclaiming
  'One Church, one Faith, one Lord'.

3

Through many a day of darkness,
  Through many a scene of strife,
The faithful few fought bravely,
  To guard the nation's life.
Their gospel of redemption,
  Sin pardoned, man restored,
Was all in this enfolded,
  'One Church, one Faith, one Lord'.

4

Thy mercy will not fail us,
  Nor leave thy work undone;
With thy right hand to help us,
  The victory shall be won;
And then by men and angels
  Thy name shall be adored,
And this shall be their anthem,
  'One Church, one Faith, one Lord'.

Edward Hayes Plumptre (1821–91)
Two verses omitted

Edward Plumptre, the scholarly Dean of Wells Cathedral, wrote this hymn towards
the end of his life. He entitled it 'Church Defence'. The critics and cynics of his day
were suggesting that the Church (meaning in particular the Church of England) was
a failure and its days were numbered.

In his hymn the dean defends the Church by tracing in its long history the guiding
hand of God. He has never left himself without witness. Even in the darkest days he
has had his good and faithful servants, and from age to age the same unfailing truth
has been proclaimed: *One Church, one Faith, one Lord.*

95 *To God be the glory*

To God be the glory! great things he hath done!
So loved he the world that he gave us his Son,
Who yielded his life an atonement for sin,
And opened the life-gate that all may go in.

Praise the Lord! Praise the Lord!
Let the earth hear his voice!
Praise the Lord! Praise the Lord!
Let the people rejoice!
O come to the Father, through Jesus the Son:
And give him the glory! Great things he hath done!

2

O perfect redemption, the purchase of blood!
To every believer the promise of God;
The vilest offender who truly believes,
That moment from Jesus a pardon receives.

3

Great things he hath taught us, great things he hath
   done,
And great our rejoicing through Jesus the Son:
But purer and higher and greater will be
Our wonder, our transport, when Jesus we see.

Frances Jane van Alstyne (Fanny Crosby) (1820–1915)

Fanny Crosby, though blind, was a prolific writer of gospel songs (see 'Blessed assurance', no. 13). Strangely enough the present song was almost forgotten in the United States until recent years. Then, having become popularized in Britain and Australia through the Billy Graham crusades, it found its way back to America, where it is now a top favourite.

A hymn of this type depends a lot on its tune. This one was the work of an expert in this field, W. H. Doane (1832–1916). Though no more than an amateur musician he composed over two thousand tunes, many of them to words by his friend Fanny Crosby.

96 *We have a gospel to proclaim*

We have a gospel to proclaim,
    good news for men in all the earth;
The gospel of a Saviour's name:
    we sing his glory, tell his worth.

2

Tell of his birth at Bethlehem
    not in a royal house or hall
But in a stable dark and dim,
    the Word made flesh, a light for all.

3

Tell of his death at Calvary,
 hated by those he came to save,
In lonely suffering on the Cross;
 for all he loved his life he gave.

4

Tell of that glorious Easter morn:
 empty the tomb, for he was free.
He broke the power of death and hell
 that we might share his victory.

5

Tell of his reign at God's right hand,
 by all creation glorified.
He sends his Spirit on his Church
 to live for him, the Lamb who died.

6

Now we rejoice to name him King:
 Jesus is Lord of all the earth.
This gospel-message we proclaim:
 we sing his glory, tell his worth.

Edward J. Burns (b. 1938)

A welcome hymn by a contemporary writer. Edward Burns, a Lancashire clergy-man, wrote it in 1968 in connection with a diocesan 'call to mission'. Mission of necessity demands a message, and this is what the hymn is all about.

It not only affirms that the Church has a gospel to preach. It goes further and spells out the essence of the message. The gospel is good news, not good advice; good news of Christ and what he has done for all mankind by his birth, death, resurrection, and exaltation.

There is a lot of theology in the hymn, but it is mercifully free from obscure and pious jargon.

97 *We plough the fields, and scatter*

We plough the fields, and scatter
  The good seed on the land,
But it is fed and watered
  By God's almighty hand;
He sends the snow in winter,
  The warmth to swell the grain,
The breezes and the sunshine,
  And soft refreshing rain.

  All good gifts around us
    Are sent from heaven above;
  Then thank the Lord, O thank the Lord,
    For all his love.

2

He only is the maker
  Of all things near and far;
He paints the wayside flower,
  He lights the evening star;
The winds and waves obey him,
  By him the birds are fed;
Much more to us, his children,
  He gives our daily bread:

3

We thank thee then, O Father,
  For all things bright and good,
The seed-time and the harvest,
  Our life, our health, our food;
Accept the gifts we offer
  For all thy love imparts,
And, what thou most desirest,
  Our humble, thankful hearts:

Matthias Claudius (1740–1815)
Tr. Jane M. Campbell (1817–78)

This popular harvest hymn, like its tune, comes from late-eighteenth-century Germany. Its author, Matthias Claudius, wrote no hymns as such, but in the course of a mixed career he published a lot of poetry.

This included in 1782 a sketch called *Paul Erdmann's Festival.* It portrayed a harvest celebration in a north German farmhouse, with the peasants joining in a song of thanksgiving to God for his bountiful gifts.

Seventeen years later part of this song was published in Hanover, set to the now famous tune by Johann Schulz. In this form the hymn rapidly became popular in Germany, and then worldwide. Jane Campbell, who made our English version, was the daughter of a London clergyman.

98 What a friend we have in Jesus

What a friend we have in Jesus
  All our sins and griefs to bear,
What a privilege to carry
  Everything to God in prayer;
O what peace we often forfeit,
  O what needless pain we bear,
All because we do not carry
  Everything to God in prayer!

2

Have we trials and temptations,
  Is there trouble anywhere?
We should never be discouraged:
  Take it to the Lord in prayer.
Can we find a friend so faithful
  Who will all our sorrows share?
Jesus knows our every weakness:
  Take it to the Lord in prayer.

3

Are we weak and heavy-laden,
    Cumbered with a load of care?
Jesus is our only refuge:
    Take it to the Lord in prayer.
Do your friends despise, forsake you?
    Take it to the Lord in prayer;
In his arms he'll take and shield you,
    You will find a solace there.

Joseph Medlicott Scriven (1819–86)

Joseph Scriven was a young Irish graduate whose life was shattered by the accidental death of his fiancée on the eve of their wedding. In face of this tragedy he decided to emigrate to Canada and make a new beginning as a teacher.

It was in Ontario some years later that he penned the verses of this hymn to console his mother in a time of sorrow. A friend of his, coming across the verses one day, asked him how he wrote them. 'The Lord and I did it together,' he replied.

Clearly the words were born of his own deep suffering. They are not great poetry. Their appeal lies in their sincerity and the way they speak directly to the heart of the friendship of Jesus.

99 When I survey the wondrous cross

When I survey the wondrous cross
  On which the Prince of glory died,
My richest gain I count but loss,
  And pour contempt on all my pride.

2

Forbid it, Lord, that I should boast
  Save in the death of Christ, my God;
All the vain things that charm me most,
  I sacrifice them to his blood.

3

See, from his head, his hands, his feet,
  Sorrow and love flow mingled down;
Did e'er such love and sorrow meet,
  Or thorns compose so rich a crown?

4

Were the whole realm of nature mine,
  That were an offering far too small;
Love so amazing, so divine,
  Demands my soul, my life, my all.

Isaac Watts (1674–1748)

This has been called the finest hymn in the English language. It is almost certainly the finest of the six hundred or so hymns by Dr Isaac Watts.

He published it among his hymns for the Lord's Supper, but it clearly serves a wider purpose. The text with which he headed it was: 'God forbid that I should glory, save in the cross of our Lord Jesus Christ' (Galatians 6: 14 AV).

The hymn invites us to survey the wondrous cross. That is, not simply to give it a hasty or casual glance but to contemplate it with the eye of faith and to see in it a revelation of the love of Christ. And this is exactly what the hymn helps us to do.

See also no. 65.

100 *Will your anchor hold*

Will your anchor hold in the storms of life,
When the clouds unfold their wings of strife?
When the strong tides lift, and the cables strain,
Will your anchor drift, or firm remain?

We have an anchor that keeps the soul
Steadfast and sure while the billows roll;
Fastened to the Rock which cannot move,
Grounded firm and deep in the Saviour's love!

2

Will your anchor hold in the straits of fear,
When the breakers roar and the reef is near?
While the surges rave, and the wild winds blow,
Shall the angry waves then your bark o'erflow?

3

Will your anchor hold in the floods of death,
When the waters cold chill your latest breath?
On the rising tide you can never fail,
While your anchor holds within the veil:

4

Will your eyes behold through the morning light,
The city of gold and the harbour bright?
Will you anchor safe by the heavenly shore,
When life's storms are past for evermore?

Priscilla Jane Owens (1829–99)

A favourite gospel song from America, much loved by fisherfolk and seafarers in general. Its author, Miss Priscilla Owens, lived in Baltimore and for fifty years was an active Sunday school teacher. Most of her hymns were written for children.

This one is an exception. It uses the image of the anchor, which in the Bible is a symbol of our Christian hope: 'We have this hope as an anchor for our lives, safe and sure' (Hebrews 6: 19 TEV). In a series of questions the hymn applies this to our hold on Christ, 'the Rock that cannot move' amid the storms of life.

Index of authors
and sources of texts

tr. translated by   *par*. paraphrased by   *ver*. versified by
adpt. adapted by

Alexander, Cecil Frances (1818–95)   5, 90
Alford, Henry (1810–71)   19
Alstyne, Frances Jane van (Fanny Crosby) (1820–1915)   13, 95
Appleford, Patrick (b. 1924)   52

Baker, Henry Williams (1821–77)   69, 87
Baring-Gould, Sabine (1834–1924)   61, 74
Bell, G. K. A. (1883–1958)   16
Bennard, George (1873–1958)   89
Bianco da Siena (d. 1434)   17
Blake, William (1757–1827)   9
Bode, John Ernest (1816–74)   66
Bonar, Horatius (1808–89)   37
Borthwick, Jane Laurie (1813–97) *tr*.   11
Bourne, George Hugh (1840–1925)   50
Brady, Nicholas (1659–1726)   93
Bridges, Matthew (1800–94)   20
Bridges, Robert (1844–1930) *par*.   3, 70
Brooks, Reginald Thomas (1918–85)   81
Budry, Edmond (1854–1932)   91
Bunyan, John (1628–88)   32
Burns, Edward J. (b. 1938)   96
Byrne, Mary Elizabeth (1880–1931) *tr*.   12

Campbell, Jane M. (1817–78) *tr*.   97
Carter, Sydney (b. 1915)   54
Chisholm, Thomas O. (1866–1960)   29
Claudius, Matthias (1740–1815)   97

Cosin, John (1594–1672)   18
Cowper, William (1731–1800)   28
Crossman, Samuel (1624–84)   59

Dearmer, Percy (1867–1936)   41
Dix, William Chatterton (1837–98)   6
Dudley-Smith, Timothy (b. 1926)   83
Duffield, George (1818–88)   82

Edmeston, James (1791–1867)   46
Ellerton, John (1826–93)   85
Elliott, Charlotte (1789–1871)   43

Farjeon, Eleanor (1881–1965)   58

Gerhardt, Paul (1607–76) *tr.*   70
Grant, Robert (1779–1838)   72

Hatch, Edwin (1835–89)   14
Heber, Reginald (1783–1826)   15, 35
Herbert, George (1593–1633)   44
Hine, Stuart K. (b. 1899) *tr.*   67
How, William Walsham (1823–97)   25
Howe, Julia Ward (1819–1910)   57
Hoyle, Richard B. (1875–1939) *tr.*   91
Hull, Eleanor H. (1860–1935) *ver.*   12

Kelly, Thomas (1769–1855)   86
Kethe, William (d. 1594)   4
Kitchin, George William (1827–1912)   48

Lafferty, Karen (b. 1943)   80
Littledale, Richard Frederick (1833–90) *tr.*   17
Lyte, Henry Francis (1793–1847)   1, 76

Marriott, John (1780–1825)   92
Matheson, George (1842–1906)   68
Monsell, John Samuel Bewley (1811–75)   24, 73

Moultrie, Gerard (1829–85) *tr.*   47

Neale, John Mason (1818–66) *tr.*   63
Neander, Joachim (1650–80)   3, 78
Newbolt, Michael Robert (1874–1956)   48
Newman, John Henry (1801–90)   45, 77
Newton, John (1725–1807)   7, 27, 36
Noel, Caroline Maria (1817–77)   10

Oakley, Charles Edward (1832–65)   33
Owens, Priscilla Jane (1829–99)   100

Perronet, Edward (1726–92)   2
Petti, Anthony G. (1932–85) *adpt.*   34
Plumptre, Edward Hayes (1821–91)   94

Rinkart, Martin (1586–1649)   60

Scottish Psalter (1650)   88
Scriven, Joseph Medlicott (1819–86)   98
Smith, Walter Chalmers (1824–1908)   38
Smith (jnr.), Leonard E. (b. 1942)   75
Stone, Samuel John (1839–1900)   84
Struther, Jan (1901–53)   53

Tate, Nahum (1652–1715)   93
Temple, Sebastian   56
Thring, Godfrey (1823–1903)   20
Toplady, Augustus Montague (1740–78)   79
Traditional   26, 56

Walworth, Clarence Alphonsus (1820–1900)   34
Waring, Anna Laetitia (1823–1910)   39
Watts, Isaac (1674–1748)   42, 65, 99
Wesley, Charles (1707–88)   8, 31, 40, 49, 55, 64, 71
Whiting, William (1825–78)   22
Whittier, John Greenleaf (1807–92)   21, 62
Williams, William (1716–91)   30

Willis, Love Maria (1824–1908)   23
Winkworth, Catherine (1827–78), *tr.*   60, 78

Xavier, Sister M. (1856–1917)   51

Index of first lines and titles

Abide with me; fast falls the eventide   1
All hail the power of Jesus' name   2
All my hope on God is founded   3
All people that on earth do dwell   4
All things bright and beautiful   5
Alleluia! sing to Jesus   6
Amazing grace (how sweet the sound)   7
And can it be that I should gain   8
And did those feet in ancient time   9
At the name of Jesus   10

Be still, my soul: the Lord is on thy side   11
Be thou my Vision, O Lord of my heart   12
Blessed assurance, Jesus is mine   13
Breathe on me, Breath of God   14
Brightest and best of the sons of the morning   15

Christ is the King! O friends rejoice   16
Come down, O Love divine   17
Come, Holy Ghost, our souls inspire   18
Come, ye thankful people, come   19
Crown him with many crowns   20

Dear Lord and Father of mankind   21

Eternal Father, strong to save   22

Father, hear the prayer we offer   23
Fight the good fight with all thy might   24
For all the saints who from their labours rest 25

Give me joy in my heart, keep me praising   26
Glorious things of thee are spoken   27
God moves in a mysterious way   28
Great is thy faithfulness, O God my Father   29
Guide me, O thou great Jehovah   30

Hail the day that sees him rise   31
He who would valiant be   32
Hills of the north, rejoice   33
Holy God, we praise thy name   34
Holy, holy, holy, Lord God Almighty   35
How great thou art (O Lord my God)   67
How lovely on the mountains (*Our God reigns*)   75
How sweet the name of Jesus sounds   36

I danced in the morning (*Lord of the Dance*)   54
I heard the voice of Jesus say   37
Immortal, invisible, God only wise   38
In heavenly love abiding   39

Jesu, lover of my soul   40
Jesus, good above all other   41
Jesus shall reign where'er the sun   42
Just as I am, without one plea   43

King of glory, King of peace   44

Lead, kindly light, amid the encircling gloom   45
Lead us, heavenly Father, lead us   46
Let all mortal flesh keep silence   47
Lift high the cross, the love of Christ proclaim   48
Living Lord (Lord Jesus Christ)   52
Lo! he comes with clouds descending   49
Lord, enthroned in heavenly splendour   50
Lord, for tomorrow and its needs   51
Lord Jesus Christ (*Living Lord*)   52
Lord of all hopefulness, Lord of all joy   53
Lord of the Dance (I danced in the morning)   54

Love divine, all loves excelling 55

Make me a channel of your peace 56
Mine eyes have seen the glory of the coming of the Lord 57
Morning has broken 58
My song is love unknown 59

Now thank we all our God 60
Now the day is over 61

O brother man, fold to thy heart thy brother 62
O come, O come, Emmanuel 63
O for a thousand tongues to sing 64
O God, our help in ages past 65
O Jesus, I have promised 66
O Lord my God (*How great thou art*) 67
O Love that wilt not let me go 68
O praise ye the Lord! praise him in the height 69
O sacred head, sore wounded 70
O thou who camest from above 71
O worship the King, all glorious above 72
O worship the Lord in the beauty of holiness 73
On a hill far away (*The old rugged cross*) 89
Onward, Christian soldiers 74
Our God reigns (How lovely on the mountains) 75

Praise, my soul, the King of heaven 76
Praise to the Holiest in the height 77
Praise to the Lord, the Almighty, the King of creation 78

Rock of ages, cleft for me 79

Seek ye first the kingdom of God 80
Spirit of God, in all that's true I know you 81
Stand up, stand up for Jesus 82

Tell out, my soul, the greatness of the Lord 83
The Church's one foundation 84

The day thou gavest, Lord, is ended 85
The head that once was crowned with thorns 86
The King of love my Shepherd is 87
The Lord's my Shepherd, I'll not want 88
The old rugged cross (On a hill far away) 89
There is a green hill far away 90
Thine be the glory, risen, conquering Son 91
Thou whose almighty word 92
Through all the changing scenes of life 93
Thy hand, O God, has guided 94
To God be the glory! great things he hath done 95

We have a gospel to proclaim 96
We plough the fields, and scatter 97
What a friend we have in Jesus 98
When I survey the wondrous cross 99
Will your anchor hold in the storms of life 100